Sonar in Fisheries
—A Forward Look

Sonar in Fisheries
—A Forward Look

by D. G. Tucker
Professor and Head of Department of
Electronic and Electrical Engineering
University of Birmingham

Fishing News (Books) Limited
110 Fleet Street, London, E.C.4

A PIONEER
OF FISHERY RESEARCH

Frank Buckland 1826–1880

**This is a Buckland Foundation
Book—One of a series providing
a permanent record of annual
lectures maintained by a bequest
of the late Frank Buckland**

Printed by The Whitefriars Press Limited, London and Tonbridge

Contents

List of Illustrations

8   *Sonar in Fisheries*

Change in Terminology

It is necessary to give this warning to readers concerning a change in terminology.

The terminology for "cycles/sec" "c/s" and "kc/s" which has been in current use up to the present time has now been changed by agreement of the various engineering institutions in Great Britain to the following "Hertz", "Hz" and "kHz" respectively.

Prof. Tucker had prepared his manuscript for this book before the change was made and of course, used the terms current at the time. After full consideration it has been decided to retain the familiar terms for this book—this for two reasons. First that to change the terms now would involve the use of terms totally unfamiliar to the great majority of readers and so create confusion. The second reason is that in his recently published book *Underwater Observation Using Sonar* Prof. Tucker used the terminology hitherto current and as that book was conceived to be a companion volume and, as it were, a foundation for this book, a change would be doubly confusing.

Readers will please therefore, note the position. Not all will agree that the change in terminology is for the best: meantime for this book it is to be noted that the old terminology is retained and as and when the new terminology wins complete acceptance readers will be able to make the mental change necessary.

Foreword

Until very recently fishermen, like fisheries scientists, were literally "working in the dark": both as regards locating fish shoals and catching them. Recently, research has devised methods of underwater photography and television on the one hand, and underwater acoustics on the other, which are transforming the situation. It is particularly the latter, in the form of the conventional echo sounder, which has been adopted with enthusiasm by fishermen for both navigation and fish location; but "sonar" (as it is loosely termed) is capable of much greater development.

In this book an eminent engineer, Professor D. G. Tucker of the Department of Electronic and Electrical Engineering in the University of Birmingham, outlines current research and tells us something of the directions in which it is moving. The book itself is the final product of the "Lectures" which the Trustees of the Buckland Foundation invited him to give in 1966 in London, Hull and Grimsby. Frank Buckland, the Founder, was a far-seeing man and his bequest has provided us with a number of useful surveys of different aspects of fisheries science. It is doubtful whether any would have interested him more, or have opened his eyes more, than this endeavour to show us the methods and prospects of improved "seeing in the dark".

C. E. Lucas
Chairman, Trustees to the Buckland Foundation

Preface

Sonar is a system of "seeing" by the use of sound waves instead of the light waves used in normal vision. It has particular advantages for underwater observation because light suffers severe losses in even the clearest water and in comparison with optical systems, sonar offers relatively long ranges of observation (up to a mile or more) with much smaller dependence on the state of the water. It is not surprising, therefore, that sonar has come into general use for both fish catching and for research in fish and gear behaviour. But the equipment which has generally been used hitherto has been of a rather simple kind, and, although reasonably effective for midwater fish detection, has been rather inefficient in detecting fish very near the sea-bed and has not been adequate for the more refined observation needed for behaviour studies. However, new developments now emerging from the research stage offer immensely improved detection and observational power, and new research is being directed to still further improvement coupled with a prospect of greatly reduced cost.

The Trustees of the Buckland Foundation have been closely

in touch with this work, and although the choice of topic for the 1966 Buckland Lectures is unusual in introducing modern electronics and acoustics into a traditionally biological series, it is nevertheless entirely logical and within the spirit of the intentions of Frank Buckland in founding his Trust. It has been a pleasure to me to accept the Trustees' invitation to give the Lectures and prepare this book.

The Lectures were given in London, Hull and Grimsby during October and November 1966. The London lecture was organized jointly with the Challenger Society and held in the rooms of the Linnaean Society under the chairmanship of Dr. C. E. Lucas, c.m.g., f.r.s. The Hull and Grimsby lectures were organized by Mr. J. H. Ray, o.b.e.; the former was held in the Stratton Hall of the Sailors' Children's Society under the chairmanship of Mr. T. D. Hudson, and the latter in the Grimsby College of Technology under the chairmanship of Mr. J. Vincent. All three lectures attracted good audiences and stimulated considerable discussion.

This book represents a considerably expanded and rather more technical treatment of the subject than that given in the Lectures, but by-and-large the technical material has been kept very simple and isolated from the purely descriptive material. I have taken a good deal of trouble to explain matters in simple physical terms rather than in the more usual mathematical terms of modern engineering; but as most of the concepts involved are inherently complex it is futile to pretend that they can be understood without considerable mental effort.

The ideas described in this book are based on the work of numerous people, including present and former colleagues in the Department of Electronic and Electrical Engineering at the University of Birmingham (among whom I may particularly mention Dr. V. G. Welsby, Dr. H. O. Berktay, Dr. J. W. R. Griffiths, Dr. B. K. Gazey, Mr. J. R. Dunn, Dr. B. McCartney, Dr. J. C. Morris and Dr. D. Nairn), friends in the Marine Laboratory at Aberdeen (especially Mr. R. E. Craig), at the Fisheries Laboratory at Lowestoft, at the National Institute of Oceanography, in the White Fish Authority, in the firm of Kelvin-Hughes (especially Dr. R. W. G. Haslett) and in the Admiralty. To all these people and institutions, and to the Trustees of the Buckland Foundation and their Clerk, Mr.

F. T. K. Pentelow,* O.B.E., I must express my gratitude for help in all sorts of ways. Nevertheless, I take full and sole responsibility for the statements and opinions expressed in the book. In looking to the future I am bound to prove wrong in some matters—but I hope I am right in some too.

D. G. Tucker

Birmingham
November 1966

* It has to be recorded with regret that Mr. Pentelow died in November 1966.

Chapter 1

Sonar in Fisheries

1 Introduction

Electronics has insinuated itself into most branches of human activity nowadays, in fields as diverse as metallurgy and medicine, communications and commerce, science and Shakespeare; so it is not surprising that electronics of various kinds has also penetrated one of our oldest industries: fishing. Among the battery of electronic devices that can now be usefully installed on fishing vessels is sonar (SOund Navigation And Ranging). "Asdic" is an older British word for the same thing. Echosounders are the commonest example of sonar equipments. Strictly, I suppose, sonar depends on acoustic waves (or sound waves as they are often called—but most of them have a pitch or frequency well above the audible range) and not on electronic effects; and it probably is just possible to operate some sort of sonar system without electronics. But electronics is so bound up in the effective utilization of the acoustics that it is quite fair to include sonar in the generic term electronics. We should notice right from the beginning, however, that it is the fundamental properties of acoustic waves in the sea which control what may be done with sonar; the electronics impose practically no basic limitations.

Sonar is used in fisheries for one very good reason: it is the most convenient, economical and effective way of getting information underwater that is at present known, or indeed, likely to be known. It has serious limitations and in present forms—or in any contemplated for the future—is in no way as good as human vision in air in daylight. But human vision is poor in the dark and difficult to use underwater. For some limited purposes (albeit important in other fields of marine work) it is possible by using light waves to get results very much superior to any obtained with sonar; for instance, the gathering of detailed information about the sea-floor by underwater photography, or even about fish by either photography or underwater television. But for the type of information required in fishery operations there is really no alternative to sonar.

Fisheries operated effectively for centuries before sonar was known, and it is thus quite evident that sonar is not a basic need. But in these days of greater competition for possibly fewer fish, a device which makes the process of fish-catching more reliable and more efficient is obviously of importance. It is very necessary, however, for all concerned to decide in what circumstances sonar can be usefully applied and what type and specification of sonar is best for those circumstances.

I am sure that fishing-boat owners and skippers give a great deal of thought to this matter, and so do many of the firms that manufacture sonar equipment, and also the fisheries research scientists and engineers. Some of the information I shall recount in these lectures is of necessity secondhand, having been obtained from these sources. As a research engineer, I am primarily concerned with the generation of new ideas and the investigation of new processes in the development of sonar systems as such. I hope, therefore, that my most useful contribution will be to show what potentialities there are in sonar systems and to suggest possible benefits these may have in fisheries. Certainly there are some very much more sophisticated sonar systems coming along, and it will be surprising if some of them do not eventually find application in fisheries. And with the newer developments in electronics, like microminiaturization, there is every possibility that they will not be more expensive or larger in bulk than existing simple equipments.

It will be best to start with an examination of how the present types of sonar equipment perform.

2   Echo-sounders

The earliest form of sonar equipment used in fishing boats— and still by far the commonest—was the echo-sounder. This is a sonar with vertical beam, and its name is derived from its original, and still vitally important use in measuring the depth of water. It has been found a most useful detector of fish in mid-water and, to a much smaller extent, of fish on or very near the sea-bottom.

2.1   *Principles*

The acoustic system of the echo-sounder is simple enough in conception. A short burst, or pulse, of an acoustic wave is transmitted, and it spreads out into the water as a sort of disc of acoustic energy forming that part of a spherical sheet which is contained within the beamwidth of the transmission. Of course, an acoustic beam is not a cone with well-defined boundaries; it is really a concentration of acoustic energy which is usually greatest on the central axis of the beam and diminishes as the angle from the axis increases until eventually there is zero intensity; after that there are usually some smaller, minor, or side-lobes. But the conception of beamwidth is very convenient, and it is usually defined as the angular width of the beam between those points where the power flow per unit area (or intensity) is one-half of that on the main axis. And then for convenience in discussion we may often consider the beam as having real boundaries at this beamwidth.

The pulse travels very slowly compared with the speed of light, but considerably faster than sound in air: actually at about a mile per second. If some object which has acoustic properties different from those of water lies in its path, some of the pulse energy is reflected and spreads out from the object. Some of this reaches the receiving system and is detected and recorded through the help of the sonar equipment. The time that has elapsed between the transmission of the pulse and the reception of the "echo" is a measure of the distance or range of the object.

The electronic and electrical parts of the system perform the following functions:

(a) generate an electrical oscillation at a pre-determined frequency, and switch on a short burst of this at a suitable time,

(b) convert this into an acoustic wave at the same frequency by means of the transmitting transducer,

(c) convert the echo acoustic wave into an electrical oscillation by means of the receiving transducer,

(d) amplify the echo pulse as necessary,

(e) measure the time elapsed since the pulse was first transmitted (by means of a "time-base"),

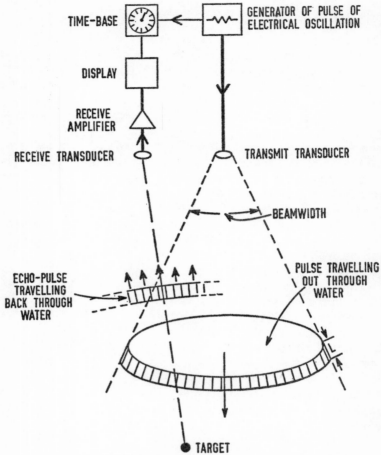

Fig. 1.—General principles of echo-sounder.

(f) display the echo pulse visually in such a way that the range of the echoing object, or "target", is directly indicated. The same transducer can usually be used for both transmitting and receiving, since these two functions are not required at the same time, by means of a correctly-timed changeover switch. In Fig. 1 an attempt has been made to show the functioning of an echo-sounder in graphic form.

One or two quantitative relationships need to be noted before we can examine the performance of the echo-sounder in a practical situation. These are given only very briefly here but are discussed in much more detail in my book "Underwater Observation Using Sonar" published as a companion volume to these lectures.

(i) If the duration of the pulse as generated is T seconds, and the velocity of propagation of acoustic waves in the water is c metres per second, then the length L of the pulse in the water is $L = cT$ metres.

(ii) The significant measure of the strength of the acoustic wave is its intensity, defined as the power flow per square metre of cross-section, and represented by the symbol I. Clearly as the wave progresses and spreads out, its intensity decreases as a square-law of distance, or by 6 dB per doubling of the range. There is, in addition, a loss of intensity due to absorption of energy (and conversion into heat) and this is very small at low frequencies (less than 0·1 dB per kilometre at 1 kc/s) but rises rapidly according to an approximate square-law of frequency (except for a kink around 100–400 kc/s) to reach very high values at high frequencies (e.g. perhaps 25 dB per km at 100 kc/s and 90 dB per km at 500 kc/s.

(iii) The target returns a varying amount of echo intensity according to its "target strength" (TS). This is defined as the ratio of the echo intensity (I_2) at 1 metre from the centre of the target, to the incident intensity (I_1). It is usually expressed in decibels so that $TS = 10 \log_{10} (I_2/I_1)$. Small targets like fish are therefore described by a target strength of a negative number of decibels. The unit target, with $TS = 0$ dB, is a sphere of 4 metres diameter.

(iv) A target without boundaries within the beamwidth, such as the sea-bottom, is defined by a strength per unit area.

(v) The limit of range for a specified target is that which makes the echo intensity at the "receive" transducer too low to be detected, however high the "receive" amplification may be made, because it is swamped by noise of various kinds (usually noise generated in the sea). The ratio of echo intensity to noise intensity, expressed in decibels, which can just be tolerated for reliable detection is called the "recognition differential" (D). For a single echo return this would be about + 6 dB, but as the pulse transmissions are regularly repeated, it is often possible to improve on this by the juxtaposition (or superposition sometimes) of successive display traces, as in the chemical recorder, so that D is reduced to say zero or even as low as -6 dB.

Items (ii) to (v) can be conveniently brought together in a very simple way in what is known as the "sonar equation":

$$2\mathcal{N} = I_S + TS - I_N - D$$

where all quantities are in decibels, and

$\mathcal{N} =$ maximum permissible one-way propagation loss between transducer and target

$I_S =$ intensity of pulse wave 1 metre from transmitting transducer on axis of beam

$I_N =$ intensity of noise at receiving transducer.

This forms the basis of design and assessment of sonar systems in general. If everything but $\mathcal{N}$ is specified, then $\mathcal{N}$ can be calculated and from this the most suitable frequency can be determined, although allowance must be made for the fact that I_N depends on frequency. If only I_S is unspecified, then from the equation I_S can be determined and hence the power required.

The significance of item (i) is in this context mainly that the pulse length in the water determines how far apart in range different targets have to be to be separated on the display. In addition the pulse duration in seconds determines what bandwidth the transducers and amplifier must have to pass it properly, since the bandwidth in cycles/sec should not be less than the reciprocal of the pulse duration in seconds.

2.2 *Detection of fish by ordinary echo-sounder*

Let us first of all ignore the effect of the sea-bottom on this problem and concentrate on how fish may be detected in general. Consider an echo-sounder with the following specification:

Frequency 30 kc/s
Beamwidth 30 degrees conical (on both transmission and reception)
Acoustic power 100 watts
Pulse duration 1 millisecond (i.e. pulse length in water is 1·5 metres)

The target strength of a fish is hard to give in exact terms; it depends on species, size, direction of view (top-view, end-on, tail-on, side-on, etc.) and other factors. But assuming the echo-sounder looks down on the dorsal view of the fish, then a herring of 30 cm length would have a target strength of about − 30 dB, and a cod of one-metre length about − 20 dB.

At 30 kc/s, the absorption loss in typical sea-water is about 6 dB per kilometre.

An acoustic power of 100 watts from an omni-directional transducer would give an intensity at 1 metre of $100/4\pi$ watts/m². The conical beam of 30 degrees width concentrates this in a ratio of approximately 60 : 1, so that the actual intensity at 1 m is about 480 watts/m². Thus I_S in the sonar equation is about + 27 dB relative to 1 watt/m².

At 30 kc/s, the noise is dominantly what is known as "sea-state" noise, and for sea-state 5 is of the order of − 140 dB relative to 1 watt/m², per cycle/sec of bandwidth. As the pulse duration is 1 ms, the bandwidth required is 1,000 c/s, which raises the noise level by 30 dB. But the received noise in the system is reduced by the fact that the receiver is directional, and only one-sixtieth of the sea noise is actually accepted by the beam. This effect reduces the noise by 18 dB. This the actual value to be chosen for I_N is − 128 dB.

Assuming a recognition differential of zero decibels, this gives, from the sonar equation:

$$2\mathcal{N} = 27 - 30 + 128 = 125 \text{ dB for a herring}$$
$$\text{(or 135 dB for a large cod).}$$

Allowing for spreading and absorption losses this gives a maximum range of detection of approximately 750 metres for a herring and 1,100 metres for a cod.

Now these ranges are somewhat larger than those normally obtainable in practice. But we assumed ideal conditions in that no allowance was made for any propagation losses other than spreading and absorption. In practice there may be other sources of loss such as thermal inhomogeneities and turbulence. And we assumed that the only noise was sea-state noise at sea-state 5; in practice there may be other noise (e.g. from water flow past the transducers and from the ship's machinery) and volume reverberation as well. (N.B. Volume reverberation is the general backscatter of the transmitted pulse from all the various particles and other inhomogeneities in the water.) We also assumed a recognition differential of zero decibels; but this would need a number of successive echo returns—probably about a dozen—to be received, and the fish might not remain in the beam long enough, due, for example, to its swinging as the ship rolls. If we allow a worsening of say 20 dB on the right-hand side of the sonar equation for all these factors, we get a maximum range of about 330 metres (i.e. about 175 fathoms) for herring and about 550 metres (i.e. about 300 fathoms) for a large cod; and these are not too far from what is actually obtained, when no special deleterious factors such as aeration of the water and other effects of very bad weather conditions are present.

These calculations show that individual fish are detectable when they are separated from one another and from other targets by at least one pulse length in depth and at least one beamwidth horizontally. If several fish are too close together for this condition to be met, then a single echo return is received, but of longer duration if the fish are at slightly different ranges—which may not mean different depths, of course, if they are in different parts of the beam. Since the beamwidth at a depth of say 100 fathoms is about 100 metres, there is a large chance of several fish being at the same range within one beamwidth. But these are instantaneous conditions. Sometimes a group of fish can be detected as separate fish by virtue of the way their range changes as they pass through the beam. This is illustrated in Fig. 2, where it is assumed that the difference (BD) between slant range at the edge of the beam and axial range is greater than the pulse length L^*. With the parameters specified, this is the case at depths greater than about 45 metres or 25 fathoms. The fish-echo traces on a recorder appear as shown at (b), and it is easily seen from this that two fish are present.

We must now proceed to see what happens when the fish is near the sea-bottom. Consider the problem as set out in Fig. 3. If there is a fish somewhere on the line between B and D, then

* Because of the two-way travel of the pulse in returning an echo, the range separation of two point targets needed to separate them on the display is ideally only $L/2$. But allowing for the finite size of the targets if they are fish, and for the rounding of the pulse envelope due to the non-infinite bandwidth of the system, it is better to think in terms of a range separation of L in order to separate targets on the display in practice.

its echo will be received before any echo from the bottom, and if it is at a height above the bottom greater than the pulse length, its echo will show on the display as a separate mark. But a fish at the same depth at the edge of the beam, say at A or C or below, gives an echo at the same range as part of the bottom echo, and since the latter is vastly more powerful, the fish echo cannot possibly be detected. Clearly it is only in

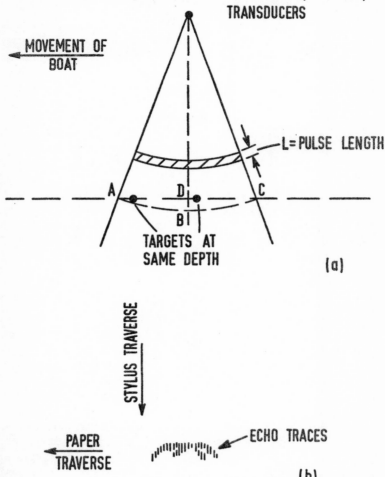

Fig. 2.—Showing how two targets (i.e. fish) at the same depth are resolved by widebeam echo-sounder: (a) geometry of situation, (b) echo traces on recorder.

the region enclosed by the line ADC and the arc ABC that fish below the height *h* are potentially detectable, and then really only provided their height above the arc ABC is greater than the pulse length. It may also often be of importance that fish above the line ADC can give echoes appearing to be very near the bottom when they pass through the edges of the beam.

A fish at height *h* would produce an echo trace as shown at (b) as the boat moves along. If the height above the bottom were reduced to the pulse length, no gap would show between the fish echo and the bottom echo. With a perfectly flat bottom and with no fluctuation in the height of the transducer due to up-and-down motion of the boat (i.e. in absolutely calm conditions), the fish would be detectable by the hump in the bottom profile. Under practical conditions, it would not be detectable. But we shall see later that the devices of the "white line" and "bottom-lock" can help greatly in this matter.

Some specimens of actual recorder chart taken at sea are shown in Figs. 4 and 5 (in first art-paper section—page 33) to illustrate the matters just discussed.

The discussions of Fig. 3 assumed a level bottom. If the bottom is sloping the matter is more complicated, and fish may be recorded as being within a certain distance of the bottom when in fact they are higher and might be missed by the trawl.

2.3   *Improvements to the ordinary echo-sounder*

The performance of the basic simple echo-sounder just discussed is certainly useful, but leaves quite a lot to be desired. A number of improvements have been brought in over the years. Some of these relate to the basic acoustic parameters and some to the method of presentation of the echoes. As all are well-known to fishing people, there is no point in going into descriptive detail. A summary of the main improvements follows.

(a) As far as the basic acoustic parameters are concerned, these have been improved by the use of higher transmitted acoustic power (several kilowatts in recent equipments), somewhat larger transducers with consequently narrower beams, and slightly shorter pulse durations to give better resolution.

(b) The earliest improvement in presentation was the

addition of a cathode-ray-tube A-scan display as an adjunct to the chemical-paper recorder. Owing to the very rapid time-base traverses possible with electronic (as opposed to mechanical) devices, it was possible to open out the display and show any part of the range in great detail. This is particularly useful

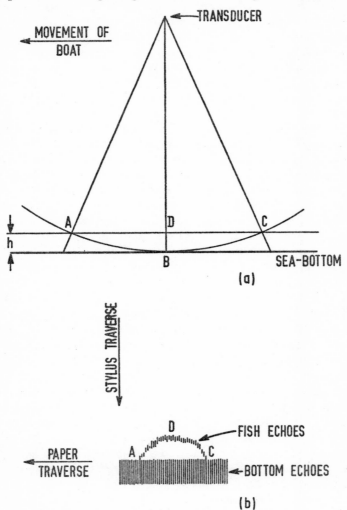

Fig. 3.—(a) Showing geometry of echo-sounder beam (b) echo-trace of fish at height *h* above sea-bottom as ship moves.

for the detection of fish very near the bottom, since the two or three fathoms immediately above the bottom—which contain the trawlable fish—can be made to occupy the whole width of the display tube. An example is shown in Fig. 6 (art section— page 34).

A disadvantage of the cathode-ray display is its very transient nature, and the paper record available in the mechanically-driven chemical recorder is often of great value in assessing the fish shoals. By very clever engineering, the recorder has recently been made capable of very high speeds of stylus traverse (e.g. 10 ms per traverse) and so able to give expanded-scale records of the bottom four fathoms as shown in the examples of Figs. 4 and 5.

(c) The difficulty which arises when the fish are within a pulse length from the sea-bottom has already been mentioned. The ordinary record taken under normal conditions shows a wavy bottom profile due to the fact that the boat is pitching and tossing, rolling and lifting, etc. and the transducer has to move with it. The bottom may be quite flat, but the depth below the transducer is what is recorded and this fluctuates. Against this wavy profile it is naturally hard to detect those fish, the echoes from which give merely a small hump on the profile.

To overcome this difficulty devices have been introduced which cause the recorder trace to indicate clearly the position of the fish above the actual bottom profile. All such devices utilize the obvious fact that the bottom echo is very much stronger than that of the fish and can therefore be distinguished by an electronic circuit which measures the echo strength.

The simplest such device is the "white-line". What happens here is that as soon as the powerful bottom echo is received, an electronic circuit applies a bias voltage to the recorder stylus so that almost instantly the recorder ceases to mark for perhaps two or three milliseconds. Thus, in effect, a white line is drawn along the profile showing the actual bottom profile. Since the electronic circuit is set so as not to be responsive to the relatively weak fish echoes, these show as marks in their proper place above the white line, as shown in the example of Fig. 4. This can be seen to be very useful in making the fish echoes detectable.

Another such device is "bottom lock". With this, the bottom echo is used as the reference for the chart and is itself merely recorded as a perfectly level, flat profile. Fish echoes show at their proper height above it. This is very valuable for fish detection. To achieve it there is the complication to be over-come that the bottom echoes which are to be used as a reference are received *after* the fish echoes. This means that some part of each pulse-return signal has to be stored for display after the bottom reference signal has been received. This makes the system a little more complex but the improvement in detection is probably worth the extra cost.

2.4 *The possibilities of narrow-beam high-frequency echo-sounders*

The rather brief examination of the performance of existing echo-sounders which I have given leads to the conclusion that severe limitations arise because of the wide beamwidth (say 30 degrees) and the pulse length which, at about 1·5 metres, is about one-third the trawlable range of fish above the sea-bottom in demersal trawling. It is not, however, reasonable to improve either of these features very greatly while retaining the same acoustic frequency of say 30 kc/s. The reasons are simple.

The beamwidth of a transducer is approximately inversely proportional to its linear dimension in units of the wavelength. measured in the plane in which the beamwidth is measured, Very approximately, provided the beam angles are not too large (say up to about 30 degrees), the beamwidth of a rect-angular transducer in the plane containing one of its main axes (i.e. parallel to one pair of sides) is given by λ/l radians. Here a radian is about 57 degrees, λ is the wavelength of the acoustic wave and l is the length of the axis. So a 30-degree beam requires a transducer dimension of 2 wavelengths. At 30 kc/s, λ is about 5 cm or 2 inches. Thus the transducers commonly used are of the order of 10–15 cm in each dimension.

If a very much narrower beam is required, say 2 degrees, then the transducer dimensions would have to be increased to about 30 wavelengths or 150 cm (about 5 feet). Such a size would be completely prohibitive on account of cost of the transducer, cost of mounting, and general awkwardness.

The pulse transmitted has desirably a number of cycles of oscillation within its length—or in more technical terms it should have a bandwidth which is only a fraction of the oscillation frequency—in order that it can pass through the transducers without distortion or destruction. At 30 kc/s, a pulse of 1 ms duration contains 30 cycles, and requires a bandwidth of 1 kc/s. It is quite feasible to reduce this pulse duration to say 0·25 ms, requiring a bandwidth of about one-seventh of the oscillation frequency. Transducers can be made to pass this reasonably well. To reduce the pulse duration below this is hardly feasible.

The solution to both these problems is, of course, to raise the frequency. But a price has to be paid for this. The absorption loss in the sea increases rapidly as frequency increases. At 100 kc/s it is about 25 dB per kilometre: at 200 kc/s it is nearer 40–50 dB per km, and at 300 kc/s it is about 50–70 dB per km. So the range of detection may be seriously reduced. It is clearly necessary to assess the matter properly.

What is a reasonable requirement for beamwidth? This is a most difficult question. One factor which must be decided very early is whether the beam is to be allowed to swing about as the boat rolls and pitches and yaws (as it does with the ordinary wide-beam echo-sounder) or whether the expense of stabilization of the beam can be justified. Stabilization can be effected either by mounting the transducers in gymbals with an electric-motor drive or by deflecting the beam electronically; in both cases the controlling signals come from a gyro installed in the boat.

Fig. 4.—(*Opposite*). The lower photograph shows an echo-sounder chart in which a large number of individual fish can be detected by the black arcs formed by their echoes as explained in connection with Figs. 2 and 3. The distance from the upper edge to the lower edge corresponds to 120 metres. The "white-line" device has been applied to this record, and the true profile of the sea-bottom is represented by the thin black line immediately above the white area. Fish very close to the bottom are seen clearly.

The upper photograph shows a scale-expanded record of exactly the same signals; the distance from upper to lower edges here corresponds to only the 8 metres immediately above the bottom as "bottom-lock" is applied. The fish very close to the bottom are very distinct.

(Courtesy Kelvin Hughes, a Division of Smiths Industries Limited)

Fig. 5.—(*Opposite*). The photographs here show another pair of "white-line" (lower) and "scale-expanded" (upper) records as shown in Fig. 4. In this case, however, it is comparatively difficult to detect the presence of fish very near the sea-bottom on the normal record with 120 metres range—even with the help of "white-line". But with the scale-expanded record detection of these fish is very clear.

(Courtesy Kelvin Hughes, a Division of Smiths Industries Limited)

33

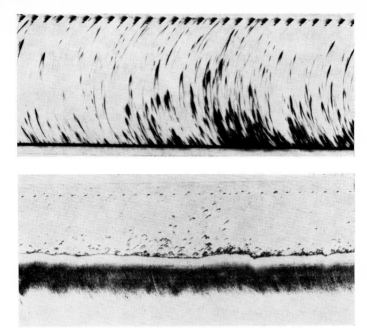

Fig. 4.

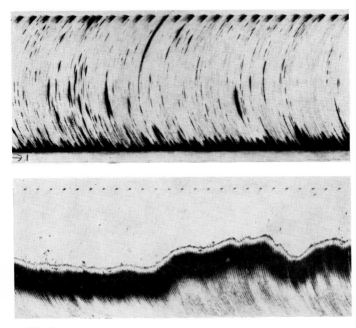

Fig. 5.

34

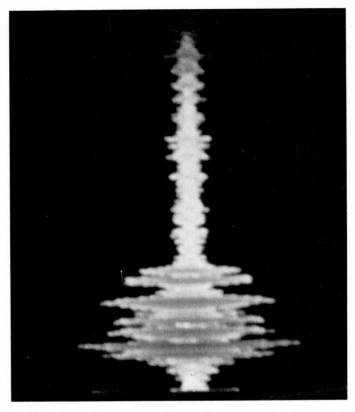

Fig. 6.—Cathode-ray A-scan display showing the range of 20 metres immediately above the sea-bottom as seen with an echo-sounder. A shoal of fish extending up to about 6 metres above the bottom is clearly indicated by the width of the trace. Above this the varying width of the trace probably represents only noise picked up in the system.

(Courtesy Kelvin Hughes, a Division of Smiths Industries Limited)

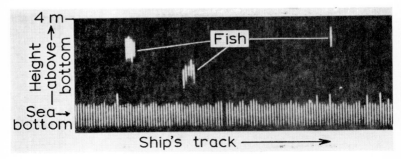

Fig. 8.—Special recording (using film and cathode-ray display) showing fish close to sea-bottom as detected by high-frequency narrow-beam echo-sounder with "bottom-lock".

(Courtesy Marine Laboratories, Aberdeen)

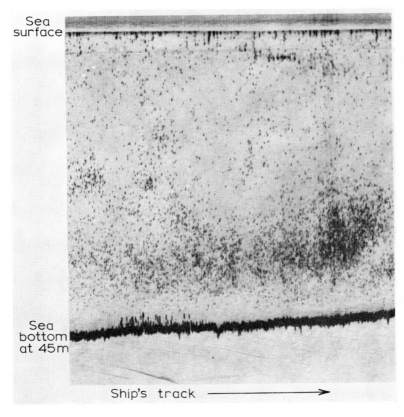

Fig. 7.—Recorder trace obtained with 400 kc/s echo-sounder having pencil beam of about 2 degrees beamwidth. The clear recording of fish is obvious, even of those within 2 metres or so of the bottom.

(*Courtesy Marine Laboratories, Aberdeen*)

36

Fig. 11.—Many fishing sonars are equipped with both horizontal and vertical beams which can be selected at will, and this record was obtained with such a set. It proceeds from the lower edge upwards. At first a horizontal beam of about 10 degrees width is used and it can be seen how a fish shoal is detected at the full range of the chart (1000 metres). As the boat proceeds, the range is reduced until the fish are nearly underneath the boat. Then the set is switched to the 20-degree vertical beam and the echo-sounder record of the shoal immediately below the boat is clearly seen, with the sea-bed echo on the right. (Zero range is on the left of the chart.)

(Courtesy Kelvin Hughes, a Division of Smiths Industries Limited)

There is little doubt that a beam of less than 10 degrees must be stabilized. Once it is decided to stabilize it, an accuracy of stabilization of less than 1 degree is readily obtainable. Thus, from this point of view, a beamwidth down to 1 degree is feasible. If we wish to specify the maximum transducer dimension as say 1 foot (30 cm), then a beamwidth of 1 degree can be obtained by going up in frequency to get 60 wavelengths in this dimension, i.e. $\lambda = 0.5$ cm and frequency $= 300$ kc/s. A beamwidth of 2 degrees is obtained at 150 kc/s.

Operationally, a beamwidth of 1 degree will just embrace a cod of 1 m length at a depth of 30 fathoms. At this depth, therefore, a reasonable estimate of size of target might even be made. The pulse duration can be as low as 0.1 ms, or even less, which gives a length of 15 cm or 6 inches, which certainly will resolve individual fish in depth. This sounds attractive.

If we then specify the new echo-sounder thus:

Frequency 300 kc/s
Beamwidth 1 degree conical
Acoustic power 100 watts
Pulse duration 0.1 ms

we find that with the same reference quantities as before the quantities in the sonar equation are

$$I_S = + 56 \text{ dB}$$
$$I_N = - 155 \text{ dB}$$

(N.B. The noise level in a 1 c/s bandwidth has been taken as $- 147$ dB for omnidirectional reception.)

$$TS = - 20 \text{ dB for herring}$$
$$- 10 \text{ dB for cod}$$

(N.B. The target strength is believed to rise with frequency roughly in linear proportion.)

We also take D as $+ 6$ dB here, since the very narrow beam-width will not permit more than one echo pulse to be received from a fish as the boat moves over it.

Then $N = 94$ dB for cod
and 89 dB for herring

which, taking the absorption loss as 0.07 dB/metre, gives a range of 500 m for herring and 550 m for cod, i.e. depths of about 270 and 300 fathoms respectively.

It is most necessary to remember that this result is for ideal conditions. At this frequency, losses are very variable, and perhaps only 100–150 fathoms could be obtained in practice. The figures obtained are not all that much inferior to those obtained for the ordinary 30-degree, 30 kc/s echo-sounder, and the increased loss has been partly compensated by the very much higher concentration (or directivity) of the beam.

The probability of the beam contacting a fish is of course reduced by the narrowness of the beam, but it seems probable that if the shoal is dense enough to be worth trawling for then adequate fish will be observed.

Preliminary trials have been carried out with a narrow-beam high-frequency echo-sounder by the Marine Laboratory at Aberdeen and the results were very promising, see Figs. 7 and 8 (art section—pp. 34 and 35). Further development is now being sponsored by the White Fish Authority and the results of extensive operational trials by fishing boats are awaited with interest. I am not at present quite sure that the case will be overwhelmingly in favour of the narrow beam in view of the greater expense involved in stabilization. The narrow beam may not be advantageous in detecting fish, but it should certainly help in assessing the density of a shoal and perhaps in indicating the size of the fish.

3   Sonar systems with non-vertical beams

There has been in the last decade or so a very considerable development in the use of sonars with beams which may be used in positions very far from the vertical—even horizontally —and which may be "trained" mechanically to point in any desired direction in both vertical and horizontal planes. The object of such systems is to permit the detection and location of fish at some distance from the boat horizontally, not only to increase the area and speed of search but also to detect the fish ahead of the boat's arrival over them and to permit, in suitable cases, nets to be placed around them accurately. Typically the beamwidth in such a system is of the order of 5 degrees. One particular commercial equipment (the "Explorator") has a frequency of 61 kc/s, a beam which is approximately elliptical in cross-section and, when horizontal, has a vertical beamwidth of 2 degrees and a horizontal beamwidth of 10 degrees, and a pulse duration adjustable from 1 to 30 milliseconds. Although the transmitted power is not mentioned in the published description, regular detection of fish is claimed near the bottom in depths of 60–100 fathoms with the beam 20 degrees from the horizontal. This is a range of the order 350–550 metres, although exceptional detection up to 1,200 metres is also claimed. Allowing for the increased directivity of the beam compared with the 30-degree echo-sounder, and for the increased absorption loss in the water at 61 kc/s, we see that these ranges are roughly in accord with our previous calculations. Thus detection of fish in those parts of the beam which are clear of the sea-bottom may be taken to be satisfactory, and such an equipment can be expected to be of great assistance in pelagic fishing with drift-nets, seine-nets and mid-water trawls.

When we come to consider the detection of fish for demersal fishing, where only those fish within two or three fathoms above the bottom are of concern, the situation is much more complicated. Consider a beam at an angle intermediate between horizontal and vertical, as shown in Fig. 9. Up to the range limited by the dashed arc in the diagram, any fish in the beam may be detected if its echo is sufficiently strong compared with the background of noise from the sea (and, in exceptional conditions, also sufficiently strong compared with any random scattering of the acoustic wave from particles, plankton, etc. in the water—known as volume reverberation and frequently negligible). But the echo from any fish within the shaded region beyond the dashed arc is received simultaneously with the returns (or back-scattering) from the sea-bottom. Generally this back-scattering, or "bottom reverberation" as it is usually called, is at a very much higher level than the fish echo, which therefore cannot be detected.

If h is the height above the sea-bottom above which fish cannot be caught by the trawl, then the only fish of interest which can be detected at the moment to which the diagram refers are those contained in the small region of the beam which is marked by stippling.

Now the diagram of Fig. 9 is an idealization of the conditions. We must remember that the beam does not have sharp boundaries, and that the lines drawn merely indicate the width between the directions where the power response on transmission has fallen to one-half of that on the central axis. There is still some power transmitted outside the nominal beam. Similarly on reception, the same directional response applies

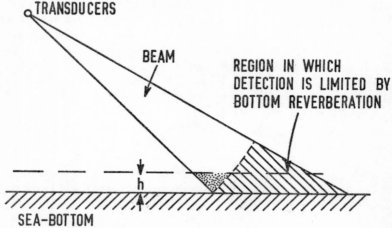

Fig. 9.—Showing how bottom reverberation limits the range of clear detection of fish.

(assuming receiving and transmitting transducers are identical). The overall directional response is the product of the transmitting and receiving responses, so that the overall beamwidth between half-power directions is less than that for each transducer separately, and it is therefore best to regard the nominal beamwidth of the system as that of the overall directional response. But there will still be some response outside this beamwidth, a typical overall directional response (for a plain rectangular transducer design with uniform sensitivity over all its active surface) being shown in Fig. 10.

Thus with a real beam there will be some return from the bottom on the lower side of the beam at ranges which will interfere with any fish echo from the stippled region. How serious this will be depends on the strength of the bottom reverberation. We can take a typical figure for bottom reverberation, measured as a target strength per square metre for a beam making an angle of 30 degrees to the bottom, as about − 25 dB (for a not very rough bottom). If the transverse beamwidth is 5 degrees and the depth 100 metres, and the pulse length in the water 1·5 metres, the area of bottom from which reverberation comes at any instant is about 30 sq. metres,* so that the total reverberation strength is about − 10 dB. This is considerably above the target strength of a fish, as we supposed earlier, so that no detection is possible in the shaded region. But below the nominal beam the response

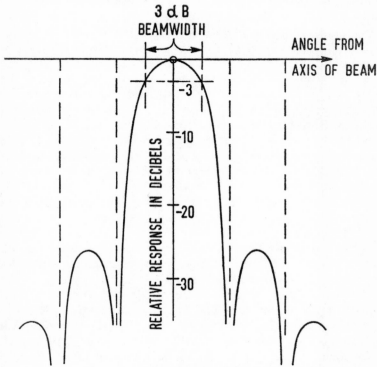

Fig. 10.—Typical overall directional response.

falls off rapidly, and from Fig. 10 we can see that a representative figure might well be 10 or 20 dB below the main response.

* The basis of this calculation may not be immediately obvious; it looks too slick! At any instant at the receiver the reverberation comes from a strip of bottom between the positions where the leading edge of the pulse arrived at the half-way time between transmission and reception and the trailing edge arrived one-half of the pulse-duration later. Thus the reverberation length along the axis of the beam is one-half of the pulse length. But as the beam is inclined at 30 degrees to the bottom, the reverberation length on the bottom is greater by a factor of sec 30°, i.e. by a factor of 2.

The fish in the stippled region are still in the main part of the beam, so the echo strength from the fish may easily be at least comparable with reverberation and in favourable circumstances will exceed it. Thus the fish in this region may well remain detectable.

It might too be argued that we could regard the beam boundaries in Fig. 9 as the directions intermediate between those of zero response and those of half-power response. This representation makes clearer the idea that there are regions where the fish are detectable. Let us tentatively accept this conclusion.

If the beam is, in plan view, pointing directly ahead of the boat and the boat is steaming along, then the stippled region of the beam (which has, of course, the full transverse width of the beam) eventually covers all the bottom area ahead of the boat, and any fish within the height *h* can be observed. This may be a perfectly satisfactory performance and may account for the claims that equipment of this kind is successful in increasing trawl catches. The system is not so useful in all-round searches and probably embraces fewer detectable fish in this method than in a simple vertical-beam echo-sounder role; but the wide area of search is no doubt valuable in itself. I do not think that any boats rely entirely on a non-vertical beam system for fish finding, but that all such systems are supplemented by an ordinary echo-sounder.

A typical recorder trace showing fish detected by a non-vertical beam is shown in Fig. 11 (art section—page 36).

The value of the non-vertical beam clearly depends very greatly on the operational procedures of fishing. If the trawl, once down, is merely towed for ten miles or so in a fairly straight line, then information obtained from the sonar during the tow is of little value anyway, except for assessing the probable amount of the catch. Its value must lie mainly in its use for a preliminary survey of the potentialities of an area. I must leave further discussion of this to the experts.

To sum up this section, non-vertical beams are of obvious value in mid-water fishing, but with present designs are of more questionable value in bottom trawling.

4   The requirements for a worth-while advance in sonar systems for demersal fishing

We have just seen that existing designs of non-vertical-beam sonars leave a great deal to be desired in regard to their use in demersal (or bottom) fishing. What is needed to make them really valuable?

One approach is this. The main limitation, as we have seen, is the bottom reverberation, which has an effective target strength over the beamwidth very much higher than the target strength of any individual fish, and thus completely obliterates any fish echoes from the region where fish and bottom are in the same range interval. One obvious possibility is therefore to make the beam so narrow in the transverse direction (i.e. in plan view) that the effective target strength of the bottom becomes less than that of a fish. Since we want to detect fish with target strengths down to at least − 30 dB, we should specify a bottom target strength not exceeding this value. This, for the conditions previously taken, (i.e. bottom reverberation of − 25 dB per sq metre for a beam at 30 degrees to bottom) requires the effective area of bottom from which the reverberation comes at any given instant to be only one-quarter of a square metre. This can be obtained at 100 metres depth with a transverse beamwidth of about 0·5 degree and a pulse duration of 0·1 millisec.

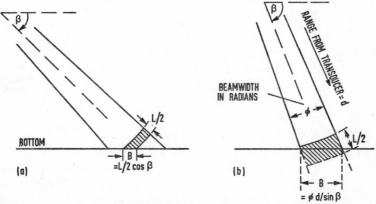

Fig. 12.—Showing (a) pulse-length-limited reverberation, (b) beamwidth-limited reverberation.

We have so far been assuming tacitly that the area of bottom from which reverberation comes is that embraced by the beamwidth in plan view and the pulse length projected on to the bottom. This situation is shown explicity at (a) in Fig. 12. There is, however, a possibility as we make large changes in the system that the rather different situation shown at (b) in Fig. 12 may apply. Here the relationship between beamwidth, pulse length and tilt is such that the intercept of the bottom in the beam is smaller than the horizontal width of the pulse. In this case the area from which reverberation comes is the whole intercept on the bottom. The two cases are called pulse-length-limited and beamwidth-limited reverberation respectively. It is clear that reverberation will be pulse-length-limited so long as

$$L/2 \cos \beta < \phi d/\sin \beta$$
$$\text{or } L < 2\phi d/\tan \beta,$$

where ϕ is expressed in radians; or in other words, so long as the pulse length is less than the beamwidth in degrees times the range, divided by 114 times the tangent of the tilt angle. Putting in some figures, take $\beta = 30$ degrees, $d = 200$ metres

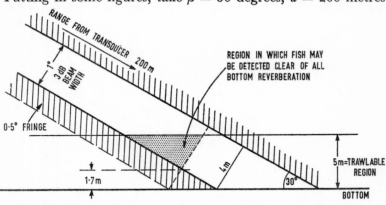

Fig. 13.—Showing improvement due to narrower beam in vertical plane.

and the beamwidth = 0·5 degree; then reverberation is pulse-length limited if the pulse length is less than 1·5 metres approximately, i.e. if the pulse duration is less than 1 ms. So in the case above, the basis of estimation of requirements was correct.

Another approach to the problem of overcoming the disadvantages of non-vertical-beam sonars in bottom fishing is to narrow the beam in the vertical plane so that most of the stippled area in Fig. 9 (where fish could be detected if it were not for the fringes of the beam) becomes free of interference from bottom reverberation altogether. This is illustrated for a numerical example in Fig. 13, which shows an enlarged diagram of the beam very near the bottom. Here a 1-degree beamwidth is assumed for the vertical plane, with a tilt angle of 30 degrees and a range of 200 metres. It is assumed that the fringe of the beam extends for 0·5 degree as shown shaded, and it is quite feasible to produce beams which have no significant response outside this fringe-width. It can be seen that the region in which fish lying in the main beam can be detected clear of all bottom reverberation extends from 1·7 metres upwards. Thus if the trawlable region is taken as the bottom 5 metres, we see that quite a reasonable detection region exists, as shown stippled in the diagram. For double the range, the vertical beamwidth must evidently be reduced to 0·5 degree.

It is advisable at this stage to look at these potential solutions to the problem rather critically so that any potential weaknesses may be exposed. There is one obvious weakness in the proposal to narrow the horizontal beamwidth in order to reduce the reverberation from the sea-bottom to a level below that of the fish; it is that in the conditions assumed above, i.e. that the area from which reverberation comes at any one instant is reduced to 0·25 sq metre, the reverberation may well not consist of a random summation of very small echoes as from grains of sand or gravel, but rather of one or two dominant echoes from large stones or even small ridges. In this case the background displayed will not be just an area of "graininess" against which the single-point echoes of fish will show up well, but instead may be composed of a number of single-point echoes from the large stones which will be indistinguishable from the fish echoes. Thus the narrow horizontal beam can be expected to work well for demersal fish only when the bottom is of fine structure and not of coarse rocky texture. However, if this method is found to be satisfactory, there is no particular virtue in making the beam very narrow also in the vertical plane; this only reduces the area of bottom examined per

transmission without improving the reverberation since the
latter is limited by the pulse duration and not by the vertical
beamwidth.

In the use of the other proposed method—the narrow
vertical beamwidth, the trouble just referred to is avoided, but
it is clear that fish just above the stippled area in Fig. 13 will
be recorded by the pulse at the same range position and there
will be no certainty that the fish are really in the bottom 5 m
or so, unless no echoes are received immediately before the
stippled area is reached. Provided the sea-bottom is flat and
level, the horizontal beamwidth which is permissible in this
method is not primarily a function of the reverberation level as
such, but rather of geometry. This arises because the beam is a
flat sector and intersects the bottom in a straight line. Thus the
range at the edges of the beam is greater than along its central
axis. It follows that fish which are much further above the
bottom than we have designed for, will be recorded at the same
range as those in the stippled area on the axis of the beam. If we
specify that fish more than 10 m above the bottom must not be
confusable with those in the stippled area in Fig. 13, (and this
may well be an over-generous concession), we can quickly see
that this limits the increase of range at the edges of the horizontal beamwidth to about 3·5 m, and that this, in turn, limits the
horizontal beamwidth to about 20 degrees if a maximum range
of 200 m is assumed, or 14 degrees if 400 m range is specified.

We made the above calculation on the assumption that the
bottom was flat and horizontal. A further restriction on
horizontal beamwidth has to be made if the bottom has a
transverse slope, because this also increases the range (still
further) at the edge of the beam which has the greater depth to
reach, and brings the bottom echoes within the stippled range
at the other edge. Taking this factor alone, assuming a maximum bottom slope of 3 degrees, and considering the same limits
and tilt as before, we find that the beamwidth is restricted to
20 degrees at 200 m range and 10 degrees at 400 m range—
almost the same figures as for the other effect. Allowing for
both factors, we see that it would be desirable to keep the
horizontal beamwidth down to 5 degrees or so in a practical
system.

It can be seen that the "Explorator" commercial sonar set

previously referred to in Section 3 approaches the figures we have here determined; with its 2-degree vertical beamwidth and 10-degree horizontal beamwidth, it approaches within a ratio of 2 or 3 to 1 of our specification for each axis.

The question of how the information would be presented in these systems is worth a thought. In both cases the use of the chemical recorder as in an echo-sounder is possible. With the narrow horizontal beam, a speckled background of reverberation from the sea-bottom will be displayed with fish showing (it is hoped!) as darker or larger marks. With the narrow vertical beamwidth, the bottom will show as a dark area as in an echo-sounder, and fish will show above it. The "white-line" technique could be applied here if desired. An expanded cathode-ray display of the echoes just above the bottom could be very useful in this case.

The conclusions we have reached are that satisfactory *acoustic* performance in respect to demersal detection may be attained only by a very substantial narrowing of the beam in one or both axes. There will be two *operational* penalties to pay, however. The first relates to transducer size, frequency and maximum range, and the second to rate of search.

We have already discussed the first matter in connection with echo-sounders, and have seen that to keep the transducer size reasonable and to work with short enough pulses it is necessary to go to frequencies like 300 kc/s, and to stabilize the transducers against roll and yaw (and probably also pitch). Our calculation showed that for a 1-degree conical beam and 100 watts of acoustic power a range of detection could be expected which even in ideal conditions would not exceed about 500 metres for herring or cod, and in practice would be a good deal less than this—perhaps only about half. An increase of power to 10 kW would increase the range by only about 100 metres at most. (A further narrowing of the beam would also increase the range.)

The question of rate of search also applied to echo sounders in so far as the very narrow beam limited the area actually sampled as the boat steamed along. But with a non-vertical-beam sonar it is presumably expected to search the area around the ship. Let us take the figures of the examples previously discussed; Fig. 13 will be useful. For the depth range,

and other parameters used there, and assuming the beam is
5 degrees wide in plan view, an area of the bottom about
8 m × 18 m, i.e. 144 square metres, is examined on each pulse
transmission. Making the extreme assumptions that only one
pulse need be used for each piece of bottom, and that just one
all-round sweep at constant tilt will be made, a ring of bottom
of about 170 m radius and including an area of the order of
10,000 square metres (or about 2 acres) will be examined in
about 22 seconds. In practice, a worth-while search at constant
tilt would require say 1–2 minutes or more. But if the boat is
steaming it may move 500 m (say one-quarter of a nautical
mile) in this time—three times the radius of search.

Quite clearly the speed of search possible with these narrow
beams is far too limited if the traditional mechanical rotation
is retained. I am convinced that the only solution is very rapid
electronic scanning of beams, in particular a system in which
the receiving beam may be swung over a very wide sector (all
of which is insonified by the transmitted pulse) during the short
period of time required for the pulse to move only its own length
in the water. Thus, instead of the pulse returns sampling the
different directions one transmission interval at a time, all
the directions are sampled during the one pulse transmission.
This will give an enormous increase in search speed. But a full
discussion of this is the subject of the next Chapter.

5   Conclusions

I have concentrated here on the detection of fish. I think it is
reasonable to conclude that existing sonar equipments are
moderately satisfactory for pelagic fishing but of very questionable value in demersal fishing. For the latter, progress will
require the use of very narrow beams and electronic scanning.

But fisheries people are interested in observing things other
than fish. In pelagic fishing, for instance, they want to observe
the mouth of the net to see that it is at the correct depth to
catch the fish. So echo-sounders are used fitted on the net
itself and measuring the vertical position of the net, the
information being relayed to the boat and displayed on the
recorder along with the fish-detection information. It would
always be useful to have a high-resolution (i.e. narrow-beam)
non-vertical-beam sonar to observe the actual net opening in

some detail. In fisheries research even more detail is wanted. A means of knowing when the cod-end of a trawl is full would be useful. And so I fancy that there will eventually be a demand for as refined sonar equipment as we research engineers can develop.

It may not always be best to use sonar equipment mounted on the ship, but instead to have it mounted on a towed body, which may be more stable and towable at considerable depths, thus increasing the depths, ranges and resolution of the observations.

I think I am safe in predicting that an era of considerable development in the use of sonar lies just ahead.

Further Reading for Chapter 1

(N.B. These papers list over 100 other references)

1 D. G. Tucker: "Underwater Observation Using Sonar", Fishing News (Books), 1966.

2 D. G. Tucker: "Underwater echo-ranging", *J. Brit. Inst. Radio Engrs.*, **16,** 1956, p. 243. (This is a substantial review paper with 66 references.)

3 R. E. Craig: "The fisheries applications of sonar", *J. Brit. Inst. Radio Engrs.*, **25,** 1963, p. 201.

4 D. H. Cushing: "The Uses of Echo-Sounding for Fishermen", H.M. Stationery Office, 1963.

5 Some examples of actual records showing fish traces as in Fig. 3 are given in the paper: E. A. Best: "Identifying Pacific Coast fishes from echo-sounder recordings", *Modern Fishing Gear of the World* 2, 1964, p. 413.

6 D. H. Cushing, F. R. Harden Jones, R. B. Mitson, G. H. Ellis and G. Pearce: "Measurements of the target strength of fish", *J. Brit. Inst. Radio Engrs.*, **25,** 1963, p. 299.

7 R. W. G. Haslett: "Determination of acoustic backscattering patterns and cross sections of fish", *Brit. J. Applied Physics*, **12,** 1962, p. 611.

8 G. H. Ellis, P. R. Hopkin and R. W. G. Haslett: "A comprehensive echo-sounder for distant-water trawlers", *Modern Fishing Gear of the World* 2, 1964, p. 363.

9 R. W. G. Haslett: "A high-speed echo-sounder recorder having seabed lock", *J. Brit. Inst. Radio Engrs.*, **24,** 1962, p. 441.

10   P. R. Hopkin: "Cathode-ray tube displays for fish detection on trawlers", *J. Brit. Inst. Radio Engrs.*, **25,** 1963, p. 73

11   J. Fontaine: "Detecteur de Poisson 'Explorator' ", *Modern Fishing Gear of the World* 2, 1964, p. 396.

12   R. E. Craig: "Narrow beam echo-sounder on trial", *World Fishing*, March 1959.

13   R. E. Craig: "Some successful experiments with a pencil-beam echo-sounder", *World Fishing*, Dec. 1959, p. 40.

14   Numerous other papers on echo-detection of fish in *Modern Fishing Gear of the World* 2, 1964.

15   D. G. Tucker and J. G. Henderson: "Automatic stabilization of underwater acoustic beams without mechanical motion of the transducer", *Internat. Hydrographic Rev.*, **37,** 1960, p. 69.

Chapter 2

The Principles and Potentialities of Electronic-Scanning Sonar

1 The difficulties and limitations of ordinary sonar systems

It was shown in the previous chapter that the direction in which sonar for fisheries is likely to develop is that of ever-narrowing beams in order that individual fish may be detected even when close to the sea-bottom at some distance horizontally from the ship's position. By means of a crude example it was shown that the price paid for this beam-narrowing in a normal sonar system is a very ineffective (or alternatively a very slow) coverage of the ground owing to the very small area of bottom which can be examined in a given time.

The search effectiveness worsens rapidly as the beam is narrowed. For the wider beams currently used in fish-finding sonars, the effectiveness is quite reasonable. This may be illustrated by the example of a beam which is conical in cross-section and has an effective beamwidth of 10 degrees. Let us assume the depth of water is 200 metres, and that the axis of the beam is tilted down by 30 degrees from the horizontal. Then the intercept on the bottom, as shown in Fig. 14, has a length of about 180 m along its long axis, and a width of about 80 m. (All our calculations will, of course, be only approximate, since the matter does not warrant very exact figures.) In plan view the intercept is roughly an ellipse as shown in various positions in Fig. 15.

A typical search procedure might well be that on which
Fig. 15 is based. Here the axis of the beam is stepped by
5 degrees at intervals equal to the time required for the pulse

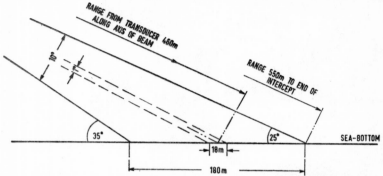

Fig. 14.—Showing the intercept on the sea-bottom of a 1-degree and a 10-degrees
beam at an inclination of 30 degrees to the vertical in a depth of 200 metres.

to travel to the maximum range and back. In this case the
maximum range involved is 550 m, and we may assume (in
order to get the most favourable result) that the pulse repetition
period can be set to 0·73 sec which corresponds to this maximum
range. If we assume the ship's speed is 8 knots (i.e. 4 m/sec)
and the axis of the beam is swung over ± 30 degrees, the
position of the beam intercept at different times is as shown in
Fig. 15, where one sweep in each direction is shown. It can be
seen that if the sweep is continued, most points on the sea-
bottom in the swept path receive altogether about four or five
pulses. It is very desirable that reliance is not placed on a
single pulse for each point, as water conditions, noise and other
factors can often result in inadequate pulse-echo returns from
individual pulses; when several are used for each potential
target position, there is a much greater probability of detecting
the target. The same result could be achieved by sweeping in
steps of 2·5 degrees instead of 5 degrees; the zig-zag coverage
would have twice the pitch and all four pulse contacts with any
point would occur in just the one sweep. From some points of
view this could be better; with a P.P.I. display,* for example,

* P.P.I. stands for "plan-position indicator". This is the kind of display normally
used in radar. It is based on a cathode-ray tube. Target echoes are presented in
their correct position relative to the transducer, as on a map.

there would be a better chance of achieving improved detection by the superposition of successive pulse returns, as described in Chapter 2 of the companion volume "Underwater Observation Using Sonar".

It can be seen that with the dimensions of the beam and of the situation as a whole which we have assumed above, the search of the area ahead of the ship is effected with completeness and it should give satisfactory results within the detection capability of the sonar. But we have already made the case that much narrower beams are really needed for proper and reliable detection of fish near the sea-floor. Suppose we repeat the above search plan with a sonar having a beamwidth of 1-degree. This beam is perhaps narrower in one dimension than is strictly required according to the calculations of Chapter 1, but is

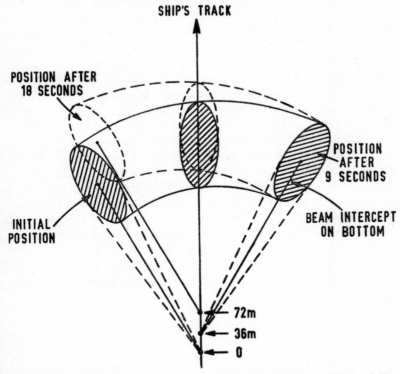

Fig. 15.—Showing bottom coverage of sonar with 10-degrees beamwidth (conical), tilt 30 degrees, depth of water 200 metres, ship's speed 8 knots.

chosen here to make the search problem clearer. The geometry of this as shown in Fig. 14 indicates an intercept about 18 m long by 8 m wide and a maximum range of only just over 460 m. If, to get the most favourable result, we reduce the pulse repetition time to 0·61 sec to correspond to this maximum range, and step the beam by 0·25 degree for each successive pulse transmission in order to get four pulses in any given line from the transducer, then the search situation is as shown by the hatched band in Fig. 16. This time it takes 2·5 minutes (instead of about 9 sec) to cover one sweep across the ± 30-degree sector. Instead of the whole area being covered, now only a narrow band is covered, about 750 m long by perhaps 12 m wide on average, i.e. a total area of about 9,000 sq. m. The total area within the nominal sector of search (the area ABCD in Fig. 16) is about 250,000 sq. m, and therefore the sonar has searched only about 2·6% of the sector. Moreover, it can be seen that instead of the nominal 4 pulses which any point in the searched area was supposed to receive, an average of less than 2 pulses is actually received because of the motion of the ship (and hence of the intercepted patch of the bottom); actually even 3 pulses are received only by points on the centre-line of the hatched band, the number diminishing towards zero at the edges. Thus, compared with the search using a 10-degree beam, this search with a 1-degree beam is only one-hundredth as effective in terms of coverage, as would be expected from the ratio of the intercepted areas of the beams. Of course, we expect that with the narrow beam most fish within the beam will be detected, whereas with the wide beam most fish may fail to be detected unless in close shoals and well above the bottom. The *overall* effectiveness of the narrow-beam sonar might thus be much higher than that of the wide-beam set; but clearly a better search coverage is very desirable. This is where a sonar system using within-pulse electronic sector-scanning comes into its own.

Fig. 16.—Showing area swept by sonar, beamwidth 1 degree (horizontally and vertically), tilt 30 degrees, depth of water 200 metres. Ship's speed 8 knots. Hatched area is swept by single-beam sonar in 2½ mins. Area ABCD is swept by electronic scanning sonar in the same time.

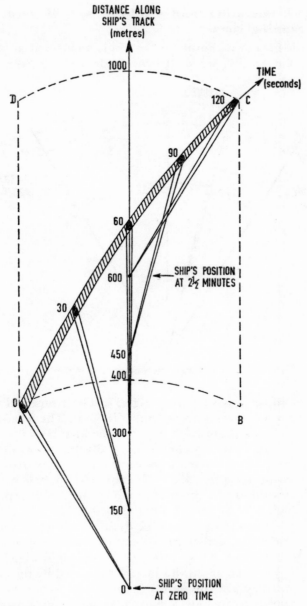

Fig 16. See caption page 54.

2   The operation and field of use of electronic-scanning sonar

The basic idea of within-pulse electronic sector-scanning sonar (which, for brevity, we shall henceforth call just "electronic-

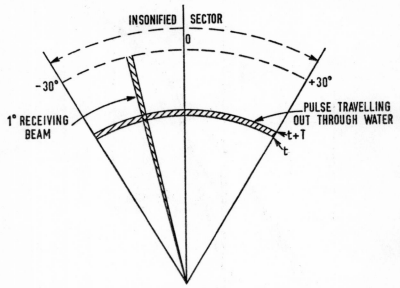

Fig. 17.—Illustrating the operation of within-pulse electronic sector-scanning sonar.

scanning sonar") is shown in Fig. 17. The transmitting and receiving transducers are now quite different. The transmitting transducer has a beamwidth equal to the angular width of the sector which is to be searched—say ± 30 degrees as shown in the diagram. The receiving transducer has a very narrow beam —taken to be 1 degree in the diagram—which can be swung right across the sector, from one side to the other, repeatedly with negligible idle time, at a high speed.

Now the transmitted pulse, of duration T sec, travels out through the water, and at any instant t forms a band across the sector, in the shape of a circular arc, as shown in Fig. 17. Any objects in this band are at this instant energized by the acoustic energy (i.e. they are "insonified"), and if the narrow receiving beam happens to include a particular object at a particular angular position, then an echo signal will be "collected" by the beam and can, after its travel to the transducer, be displayed on the display. If the receiving beam can be swung across the sector so rapidly that it covers the whole width of the sector before the pulse band has travelled its own length through the water—i.e. within a time T sec—and continues doing this repeatedly, then echo signals can be collected from all objects in the water, without any part of the sector being missed.

It is only fair to admit at this point that this picture of the operation of electronic-scanning sonar is a somewhat naive one, and that academically-speaking it leaves something to be desired. But it gives a quite adequate picture for present purposes.

It must be immediately clear that since T is likely, in practice, to be less than one millisecond, the movement of the beam through say 60 degrees in this time cannot be attained by mechanical rotation of the receiving transducer. It can be attained only by purely electrical and/or electronic means which will be described later.

Already the implications of this electronic-scanning sonar are clear. If we return to the search problem as defined by Fig. 16, we see that if the ship were fitted with an electronic-scanning sonar with the parameters shown in Fig. 17, *every* point on the sea-bottom within the search sector would be examined by a 1-degree beam once if the ship moved exactly the length of the beam intercept (i.e. 18 m) in the interval between pulse transmissions. But at 8 knots, the ship moves only 4 m/sec, and with the pulse repetition interval set at 0·61 sec as before, it moves only about 2·5 m between pulses. Thus each point on the bottom is in fact examined by seven pulses. The search effectiveness of this scanning sonar is clearly very high, and its beamwidth (on reception) allows it to detect single fish according to the calculations of Chapter 1.

It is perhaps worth pointing out, in case it is objected that the above calculation has ignored the movement of the ship between scans of the receiving beam, that this movement is quite negligible. At 8 knots, the ship moves only 4 *milli*metres during the time of scan if the pulse duration (T) is set at the maximum likely value of 0·001 sec.

It is also worth observing that provided the system is operated at shallow enough tilt angles for the reverberation to be pulse-length limited (see Chapter 1, Section 4), then there is no disadvantage in some applications in using a much wider vertical beamwidth (say 10 degrees or so) and there is the positive advantage of even better coverage.

The enormous increase in search effectiveness, coupled with detection capability, provided by electronic-scanning sonar makes it a potentially very important development for fish-finding, and it is to be hoped that it will come into general use for this purpose. But the application which has attracted most attention so far is in the study of the behaviour of fish and nets. Electronic-scanning sonars have been made experimentally, and used for this purpose, by both the author's group at the University of Birmingham and by Dr. G. Voglis and his colleagues at the Admiralty Research Laboratory, and numerous trials have been made in collaboration with the Marine Laboratory at Aberdeen and the Fisheries Laboratory at Lowestoft. There is now little doubt of the power of this new observational instrument. Results will be described in more detail later.

Electronic scanning has some obvious advantages too for hydrographic surveying, and even for ordinary navigational purposes. An echo-sounder, scanning electronically across the ship's track, will give a profile in this axis as well as in the usual axis of the ship's forward motion; thus a 3-dimensional picture of the sea-bottom is obtained. A suitable means of recording this has still to be worked out.

3   Some results achieved with electronic-scanning sonar

In the previous discussion we have concentrated attention mainly on the search problem, and have made a strong case for electronic-scanning sonar on the basis of its very high search rate. This is clearly a most important aspect of the use of sonar in fisheries. But attention must now be directed to the question of what kind of information the sonar can provide, and how it can be presented to the operator. It quickly becomes apparent that in addition to the high search capability of electronic-scanning sonar, it has the great virtue of "immediacy". By this we mean that instead of a picture of an underwater scene being built up slowly, bit by bit, as in an ordinary sonar—which means that moving objects such as fish and fish shoals may be depicted very inaccurately or lost altogether—we now obtain, virtually instantaneously, a complete picture of what lies in the scanned sector, depicted in considerable detail for every pulse which is transmitted. Thus, if we consider for the moment the ship to be stationary, then movement of fish, etc., shows up as a continuous movement of the fish shoal (or whatever it may be) across the display screen, while any fixed objects remain in the same place. If the ship is moving, the motion of fish is observed relative to the ship.

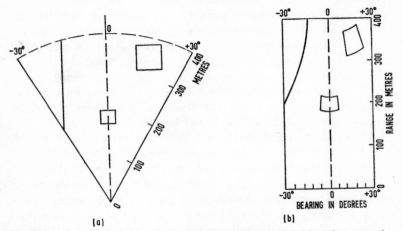

Fig. 18.—Showing the relationship between true-plan (P.P.I.) and rectangular (B-scan) display of 60-degree sector. (a) P.P.I., (b) B-scan.
The two squares and the line in (a) appear on (b) with distortion as shown.

Because of the dynamic character of the picture obtained from the electronic-scanning sonar, it is necessary to display the information obtained on a cathode-ray tube, rather as in television except, of course, that the axes are not horizontal and vertical directions in the scene observed, but instead range and bearing. Any echo received brightens up the spot on the screen, and the spot is scanned across the face of the tube so that echoes are displayed in the correct position for their range and bearing. It is quite possible to present the observed sector on a true-plan (i.e. P.P.I.) basis as shown diagrammatically in Fig. 18 (a). If this is done, and assuming the water to be shallow so that very low tilt angles are involved, and also that the beam-width in the vertical plane is not too narrow, so that a large stretch of the sea-floor intercepts the beam, then a square patch on the sea-floor appears as a square patch on the display, and a straight line appears as a straight line, as shown for two patches and one line in the figure. However, it has so far been considered preferable by those experimenting with these sonars to avoid the congestion of information which naturally occurs at the very short ranges by using the so-called "B"-scan display, which gives range and bearing as rectangular co-ordinates, as shown diagrammatically in Fig. 18 (b). This opens up the short-range part of the sector, so that all the information which the equipment gathers may be displayed clearly; but, of course, distortion of the shape of objects is caused. In the figure, the rectangular patches and the straight line parallel to the sector-axis, which appear correctly in the P.P.I. display at (a), are shown in their distorted form in the B-scan display at (b). This distortion is very rarely of serious consequence, but should be borne in mind in interpreting the results of observations illustrated below. All the display photographs and sketches here presented are of the B-scan type.

It should be noted, that it is always the range along the beam which is displayed, and that when large tilt angles are involved this "slant range" is different from the true plan range. Moreover, the beam is scanned electronically in a plane, and not at a constant tilt for all angles in the sector as would be the case if mechanical scanning could be used. These factors must be taken into account when interpreting the record of features on the sea-floor.

3.1 *High-resolution systems*

As previously stated, the emphasis in the development of electronic-scanning sonars has recently (i.e. since about 1959) been rather more for the study of fish behaviour and of nets and gear than for fish-finding in commercial operations, although earlier work by the author and his colleagues (to be described later) was concerned more with fish-finding at longer ranges. The development of high-resolution systems operating

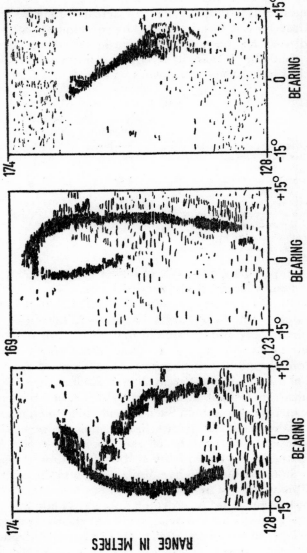

Fig. 19.—Sketches of the B-scan display of the ARL electronic-scanning sonar showing fish shoals. (*After Voglis and Cook.*)

at fairly high frequencies (e.g. 300 to 500 kc/s) with consequent rather limited maximum range (typically 100 to 200 metres) has proceeded at both the Admiralty Research Laboratory and at the University of Birmingham. The equipments with which the field work has been done have rather similar parameters (except that the Birmingham equipment works at a very economical power level), as shown in Table 1.

TABLE 1

	A.R.L. equipment	Birmingham equipment
Frequency of acoustic wave	300 kc/s	500 kc/s
Sector width of scan (azimuth)	30°	30°
Receiver beamwidth (azimuth)	0·33°	0·5°
Range resolution	7·5 cm	7·5 cm
Effective vertical beamwidth (approximately)	5°	3·75°, 7·5° or 15°
Length of receiver transducer (i.e. maximum dimension)		17 cm

Both equipments are capable of higher resolution, but these were the figures for the trials described here.

Trials carried out at sea using the A.R.L. equipment in collaboration with the Fisheries Laboratory, Lowestoft, have shown remarkably good results in delineating fish shoals and trawl nets in mid-water. Fig. 19 shows the author's sketches, made from the published photographs, of some of the better displays of fish shoals of different shapes. Each of these displays is obtained from a single transmitted pulse, i.e. in a time of less than one quarter of a second. Such sketches tend to enhance the quality of the displayed picture, but it must be remembered that single-shot photographs of the display are not really representative of the true quality of the information presented. The operator watching the live display sees a rapid succession of such pictures, and not only does this mean that echoes missed on one pulse are recorded on another, so filling in gaps, but also targets which are moving stand out clearly against any fixed background of rocks, stones, etc. It is quite impossible to convey in a printed picture any real idea of the displayed information.

Fig. 20 shows similar sketches made from the photographs

of the display when a midwater trawl was towed (by another ship) through the scanned sector of the sonar. In both pictures the shape of the trawl is clearly discernible, and in the right-hand picture the effect of the trawl on a shoal of fish is seen. Voglis and Cook, in their paper, describe how the shoal, originally single, was seen on the sonar display to divide into two as it entered the trawl mouth, the two groups moving forward separately along the right-hand and left-hand wings as shown in the sketch of Fig. 20.

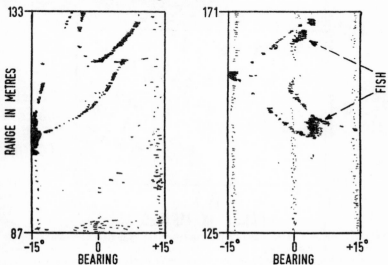

Fig. 20.—Sketches of the B-scan display of the ARL electronic-scanning sonar showing two views of a midwater trawl. On left: trawl viewed from above and behind (roughly at 45 degrees); cod-end at about 107 m on left of sector. On right: trawl viewed from above and broadside-on, showing fish shoal divided and concentrated near wings of trawl. (*After Voglis and Cook.*)

Trials using the University of Birmingham equipment have mostly been carried out from fixed stations and with the collaboration of the Marine Laboratory, Aberdeen. Although some short trials were made with the equipment mounted on a ship, at Crinan and Loch Ness in particular, these were primarily for technical tests of performance and not for fish observation. It should be pointed out that the only really significant difference between this equipment and the A.R.L. equipment lies in the size of the underwater unit. The Birmingham equipment was intended to be readily fitted to a ship, pier or tank without any special construction or trunking, and thus has a very diminutive underwater unit. The very high resolution in relation to size was obtained by the use of the higher frequency —which enables a transducer of a given number of wavelengths to be smaller in physical size—and by the use of an electronic processing system known as "multiplicative signal processing" which will be described later.

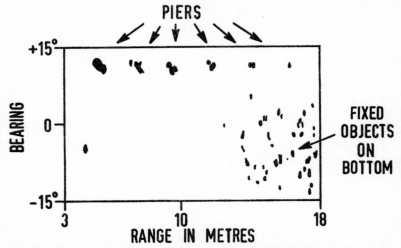

Fig. 21.—Showing three photographs (opposite) of display of Birmingham University electronic-scanning sonar used for close-range study of fish movements. The diagram (above) shows the interpretation of the fixed objects in the display. The other echoes in the photographs are small fish shoals. The photographs were taken at 5-second intervals, and the movements of the fish are clearly observable. These are day-time observations.

A practical problem of importance was studied by means of this equipment in the River Forth in front of the cooling-water intakes at Kincardine Power Station. It was required to observe the behaviour of fish in relation to these intakes. The river is extremely turbid here, making photographic observations quite impossible. The intakes are situated at the end of a jetty stretching out 200 yards from the river bank and are positioned at right angles to the tidal flow. The transducers were mounted 8 ft above the river bed and the beams directed horizontally down river so that there would be a 30-degree horizontal scanned sector with one side lying along the intakes. Fig. 21

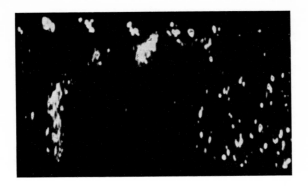

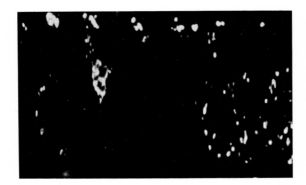

Fig. 21.—For interpretation, see caption on opposite page.

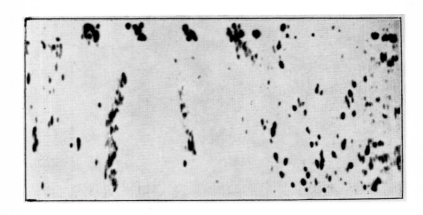

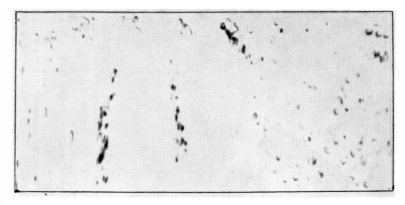

Fig. 22.—Showing the benefit obtained by cancelling-out the fixed returns in a display photograph: (a) photograph of display without special processing, (b) the same photograph after cancellation with another taken shortly afterwards.

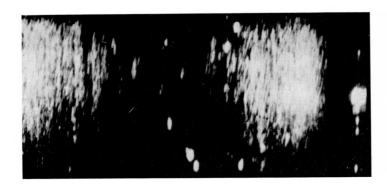

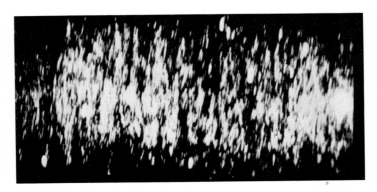

Fig. 25.—Photographs of display screen in tank experiment of Fig. 24, using 3 minutes exposure. The distribution of herring in the tank is shown: (a) in daylight, (b) in darkness.

68

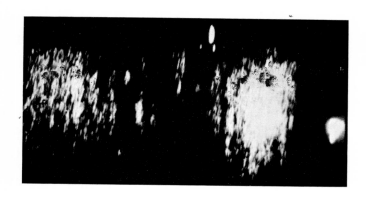

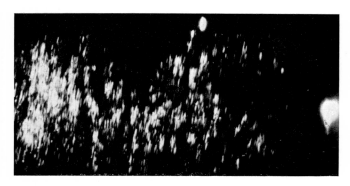

Fig. 26.—Photographs of display screen in tank experiment of Fig. 24, using one-minute exposure. The distribution of the herring in the tank is shown: (a) before switching on 100 c/s source, (b) after switching it on.

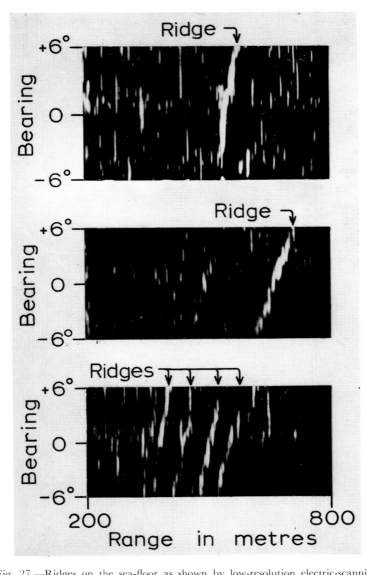

Fig. 27.—Ridges on the sea-floor as shown by low-resolution electric-scanning
sonar with nearly-horizontal beam.

70

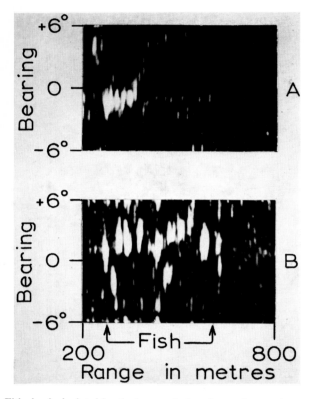

Fig. 28. Fish shoals depicted by the low-resolution electronic-scanning sonar with nearly-horizontal beam.

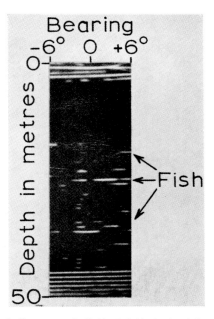

Fig. 29.—Fish (including many individual fish) depicted in midwater by low-resolution electronic-scanning sonar used with vertical beam.

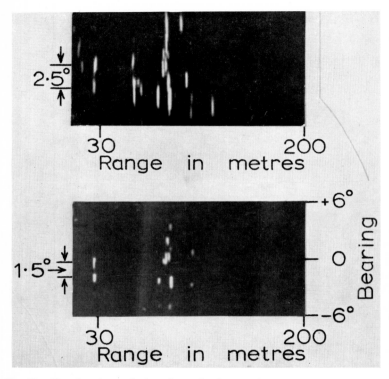

Fig. 41.—Showing the resolution of two closely-spaced targets at the same range, (8-channel scanning sonar, acoustic frequency 37 kc/s). The upper picture shows the targets just appearing separately when the angular spacing is 2·5 degrees, using the normal system. The lower picture, which was taken using multiplicative signal processing, shows that this new system enables the targets to be separated at only 1·5 degree spacing.

shows some typical results (see second art section, page 65). The diagram explains the situation. As mentioned earlier, the live display gives much more information than a few single photographs or sketches can do, but nevertheless the high resolution of the display is apparent, and the sequence of three pictures taken at 5-second intervals is sufficient to show the movement of the fish shoals (and some individual fish) in relation to the piers of the intake jetty.

The disadvantage that photographs of the display do not show the dynamic effects, i.e. the differentiation between moving objects and the fixed returns from the background, can to some extent be overcome by a technique of photographically cancelling-out the fixed returns. This is done by superposing, as transparencies, the given picture and another, taken a very short time later, which has been photographically reversed (i.e. if the first is a positive, then the second is a negative). Provided the densities are correct and that very good registration is obtained, the fixed objects disappear, but those which have moved do not cancel out (either not completely or not at all, depending on the amount of movement) and leave a clear picture of their positions. An example, taken from the same series as those shown in Fig. 21, is given in Fig. 22 (page 66), where the original and the "cancelled-out" pictures are shown together. The effectiveness of the process is very apparent. But it is still only a poor substitute for the original live display, or failing that, a ciné film of it.*

Another very interesting and important (though not new) effect which was seen in these Kincardine trials was the different behaviour of the fish at night. It is well-known that fish which form tight shoals by day tend to become spread out and diffuse by night. Fig. 23 shows a sketch of the moving fish in a typical night-time display, and the different behaviour is apparent.

Some controlled experiments on the reaction of fish to light and darkness were made using the Birmingham electronic-scanning sonar in a large tank measuring 16 m × 13 m with a

---

* At the meetings in London, Hull and Grimsby at which these Buckland Lectures were presented in October and November 1966, a five-minute ciné film of these Kincardine results was shown, including daylight and night-time sequences. The record of individual fish movements at night was especially impressive.

depth of water of 1·4 m. The layout is shown in Fig. 24, where
are also shown the arrangements for another experiment,
described below, on the reaction of the fish to a low-frequency
vibration. The fish used were herring, and in the light could be

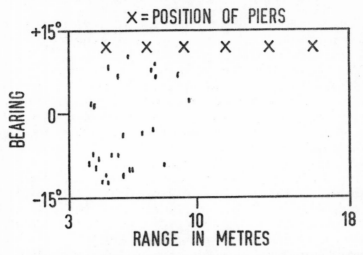

Fig. 23.—Showing the different distribution of fish by night in the same area as
observed in Figs. 21 and 22. Only the fish echoes are shown in this sketch made
from a photograph of the display.

seen to swim regularly round the tank in small groups, passing
from left to right, say, across the area marked a, . . . a and back
from right to left across the area marked b, . . . b. This movement was shown clearly by the sonar display, and was recorded
very simply by photographing the display with a very long
exposure—up to 3 minutes—thus integrating the results of
around one thousand scans of the sector. The photographs
showed clearly the concentration of the paths crossing the
sector at the two ends, with very few fish traces in the central
area between a, . . . a and b, . . . b. A typical photograph is
shown at (a) in Fig. 25 (art section, page 67).

Naturally, in the light and in the clear water of the tank,
this effect was better seen visually (i.e. optically) by direct
observation than by the use of the sonar. But to study the
behaviour of the herring in the dark, optical methods fail
completely, and the sonar really provides information other-

wise unobtainable. Direct observation of the display shows the individual fish movements. When the previous experiment was carried out in darkness, a quite different effect was displayed by the sonar, and the 3-minute exposure gave photographs of the display as shown at (b) in Fig. 25. It can here be seen that no longer do the fish swim round and round the tank

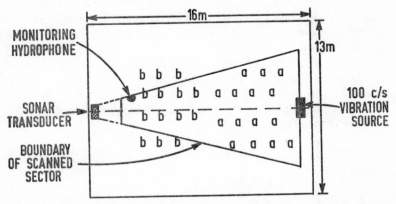

Fig. 24.—Showing the arrangement of the electronic-scanning sonar in a tank for experiments on fish behaviour in relation to: (a) light and darkness, and (b) a low-frequency vibration.

leaving the central area empty; they are now, if anything, rather denser in the central area.

The sonar was also used to study the effect on the fish, in darkness, of the low-frequency vibration introduced by the 100 cycles/sec source shown in Fig. 24. This vibration was monitored by the hydrophone shown in the diagram, and both the 100 c/s source and the monitoring hydrophone are clearly visible in the sonar displays reproduced in Fig. 26 (art section, page 68). In these photographs, a one-minute exposure was again given in order to obtain the integrating effect. The photograph at (a) was taken before the 100 c/s source was switched on, and it can be seen that the fish are gathered mainly in the region a, . . . a (as marked in Fig. 24). The photograph at (b) was taken immediately after the 100 c/s source was switched on, and it can be seen that the fish have quickly left the area near the source, and have gathered in the region marked b, . . . b in Fig. 24.

3.2   *Lower-resolution, longer-range systems*

While, as explained in the previous section, the more recent work on electronic-scanning sonar has been associated with studies of the behaviour of fish and nets, earlier work in the period 1956 to 1959 was concerned more with longer-range, lower-resolution systems of a rather simpler type. An equipment was developed and built at the University of Birmingham, with the parameters shown in Table 2, and given sea-trials, with the collaboration of the National Institute of Oceanography, in their Royal Research Ship *Discovery II* during 1958. It was these trials which first brought into prominence the potentialities of electronic-scanning sonar in the fisheries field, although its advantages as a navigational and surveying instrument also became apparent.

TABLE 2

Frequency of acoustic wave	37 kc/s
Sector width of scan	12°
Receiver beamwidth (azimuth)	1·5°
Range resolution	75 cm
Vertical beamwidth	10°
Length of receiver transducer	156 cm
Normal maximum range of detection	
of large targets (very roughly)	1000 m
ditto of single herring	300 m

Whereas the high-resolution systems discussed earlier have a very large number of receiver channels (75 in the A.R.L. equipment and 32 in the Birmingham equipment), this simpler equipment has only 8, and consequently can resolve detail across the sector only to the fineness of one-eighth of the sector width. But it is remarkable what picture quality this can give. Fig. 27 (art section, page 69) shows three photographs of the display which record very clearly some ridges on the sea-floor; here the sonar beam was nearly horizontal (actually its axis was tilted downwards by 5 degrees) and the scanning was in the azimuth plane as in all the previous illustrations.

Fish shoals show up very well with this sonar, although naturally not in the detail which the high-resolution systems can give. Fig. 28 (page 70) shows photographs of the display depicting very clearly two differently-formed groupings of fish (probably herring) in the North Sea. The large individual marks on the display each correspond to small shoals of fish; some of the smaller marks are probably individual fish, but others are fixed objects (stones, etc.) on the sea-bottom. As previously explained, the moving fish can be distinguished from the fixed objects on the live display or by examination of a film record of the display.

The electronic-scanning sonar can be usefully operated as a scanning echo-sounder by making the beam vertical and scanning in the vertical plane. A typical display photograph showing fish (again probably herring) in shallow water beneath the ship is shown in Fig. 29 (page 71). Here many of the echoes recorded must correspond to individual fish. It should be

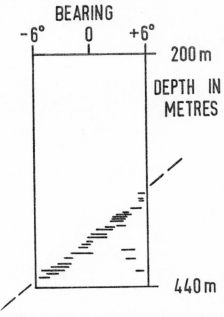

Fig. 30.—Sketch of display of low-resolution electronic-scanning sonar showing a 45-degree slope on the sea floor (continental shelf to west of English Channel).

explained that all the echoes are longer in the bearing axis than in the range axis, not because the fish are lying horizontally (although they no doubt are doing so!), but because the picture, when opened out for this very short range, has a noticeable line structure (as in a coarse television picture) which causes echoes to appear as horizontal lines rather than as "blobs"!

It has already been said that the electronic-scanning sonar can be used as a navigational and surveying instrument, and a particular illustration of its use in this role is with a vertical beam and scanning *across* the ship's track. A normal echo-sounder (in so far as it gives accurate information at all) gives only the sea-bottom profile along the ship's track. With sector-scanning across the track, the profile is also observed at right angles to the track. Naturally, a high-resolution electronic-scanning sonar with a very long range would be best for this —and one is indeed planned—but even a low-resolution equipment gives very useful results. The sketch of a display photograph in Fig. 30 shows a bottom profile taken on a single pulse transmission using a scanning sonar with only six channels, i.e. a resolution in bearing of only one-sixth of the sector width. The bottom slope of about 45 degrees is clearly indicated. A system giving this information might also be useful in fishing, although it is only fair to say that a very low-resolution system such as used for Fig. 30 would not give such good and clear results on very slight slopes, below 3 or 4 degrees say.

4   The use of electronic-scanning sonar in demersal fishing

All the experimental equipments discussed in the previous section had fairly large beamwidths in the vertical plane, relying for their resolution on very narrow receiver beam-widths in the horizontal plane. (These terms "vertical" and "horizontal" are used here in relation to a beam which has its central axis more-or-less horizontal.) For the detection of objects in midwater, or of larger objects on the sea-bottom, this arrangement is very suitable as it gives a large volume cover-age, and in shallow water a large area of bottom coverage, with good resolution due to the very short pulse-length as well as the narrow horizontal beamwidth on reception. But we saw in Chapter 1 (section 4) that for the detection of individual fish within trawlable range of the bottom very narrow horizontal beamwidths *not* also associated with very narrow vertical beamwidths, will be successful only in so far as they can reduce

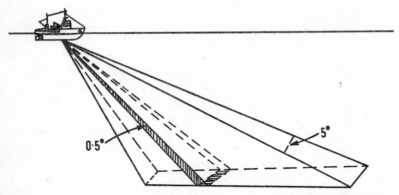

Fig. 31.—Showing use of electronic-scanning sonar with scanning in the vertical plane.

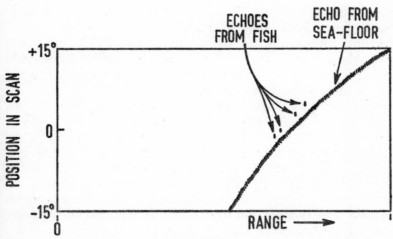

Fig. 32.—Showing the way in which echoes from fish just above the sea-bottom are displayed when electronic-scanning sonar is used according to Fig. 31.

the reverberation from the bottom to an echo-level below that of the fish; and this is a somewhat questionable matter to calculate as the target strengths of fish and sea-bottoms are not reliably known, and the assumption that the reverberation is the random addition of a lot of small echoes may fail when the intercepted area of the bottom is made very small. Thus it may well be preferable to use the alternative method, suitable for the larger tilt angles, i.e. around 30 degrees or more, using a very narrow vertical beamwidth (not necessarily associated also with a very narrow horizontal beamwidth), as illustrated in Fig. 13; this isolates at least some of the trawlable fish in a region of the beam entirely clear of reverberation. The use of extreme narrowness in both vertical and horizontal axes had better at present be ruled out as being rather impracticable, since it makes such severe demands on stabilization of the beam.

It thus appears worthwhile to consider the use of an elec-tronic-scanning sonar having its scanning action, with a narrow beam, in the vertical plane and its broader beamwidth in the azimuth plane. We saw in Chapter 1 that for a sonar with a detection range of around 400 m, using the narrow vertical beamwidth, the most suitable horizontal beamwidth was about 5 degrees. For this range, the vertical beamwidth should be about 0·5 degree, so that a suitable scanning sonar would operate as shown in Fig. 31.

It would probably be best to use a B-scan display with this system as with the others, and the echoes from the sea-floor would then show as a curved continuous line as shown in the sketch of a typical display in Fig. 32. Fish in the stippled area of Fig. 13 should show as small marks clear of the bottom echo as also shown in Fig. 32. As far as is known no operational trials have been made at sea to prove how effective this system would be in practice, but trials using the Birmingham scanning equipment have been made in the large tank and have shown good promise.

5   Fundamental principles of electronic-scanning sonar

So far we have managed to discuss within-pulse electronic sector-scanning sonar without any technicalities as to how it works. In its full development, any discussion of electronic-scanning sonar is necessarily very complicated and advanced, since the system is complex and its finer points are dependent on rather difficult academic analysis. For such discussion the published papers listed at the end of the chapter may be referred to. Here we shall attempt to explain the basic principles using as the starting point the elementary presentation of sonar fundamentals given in the author's companion volume "Underwater Observation Using Sonar". In Chapter 2 of this book the way in which acoustic beams are formed was described quite fully. Assuming this description was understood, the following account of electronic-scanning sonar should present no difficulty. It should be explained that there are many ways of achieving electronic sector-scanning; that to be described is just one way which was developed at the University of Birmingham. But many of the fundamental features are common to all.

5.1 *Outline of system*

A schematic diagram of the system is shown in Fig. 33. The receiving transducer is n times the length of the transmitting transducer, and is divided into n sections, where n is the number of beam-widths (as measured between points where the power response has fallen to half) it is desired to contain in the scanned sector. If these n sections were connected to n corresponding, uniformly spaced, taps on the delay line, then the beam would be deflected by an amount dependent on the phase-shift in the delay line. The principle of this is readily seen; if an echo is received from a target on a bearing of θ relative to the perpendicular axis of the transducer, then the wave-front of the echo pulse lies parallel to the line shown in Fig. 33. The echo is received by the first transducer section before it reaches the second, and so on. Thus the echo signal received by successive sections is delayed in phase relative to the previous sections. If a peak output is to be obtained for this particular angle of arrival, then the delay line is required to insert compensatory phase-shift so that all the components of the combined output are in the same phase.

In the scanning system, frequency-changer equipment is inserted between the transducer sections and the delay line. The local oscillator which feeds all the frequency-changers is

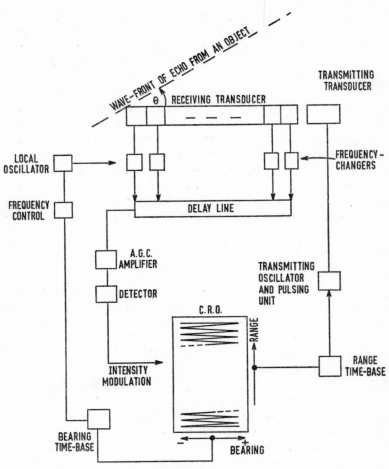

Fig. 33.—Schematic diagram of electronic sector-scanning system.

swept in frequency by the bearing time-base, so that the signal frequency received by the delay line varies over a range during every sweep of the bearing time-base. If then the delay line is made to have a phase-shift which varies over this frequency range from negative values to positive values, the beam will be swept from left to right during each sweep of the bearing time-base. The latter also deflects the spot on the cathode-ray tube from left to right, so that signals received on any particular bearing are recorded on that bearing on the display. The range time-base works in the usual way, so that the position of an echo-spot on the tube indicates the position of the echoing object on rectangular axes of bearing and range. If the bearing scan is so rapid that it is completed within the duration of the pulse and is immediately repeated, no information is lost and all directions in the sector are effectively looked at simultaneously, but with the angular resolution corresponding to the beamwidth of the receiving transducer.

5.2   *Width of the scanned sector*

It was stated above that the receiving transducer was divided into n sections, where n is the number of beamwidths it is required to contain in the scanned sector. We must now see why this is so.

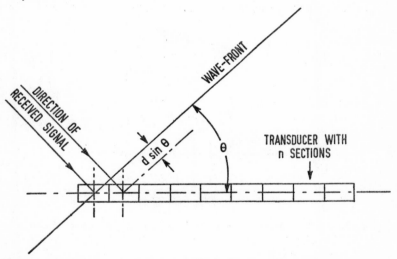

Fig. 34.—Showing a transducer in n sections and the geometry involved ($n = 9$ in this example).

Assume that the transducer is made up of n contiguous sections of length d, so that the length l is equal to nd. From the discussion in the companion volume it should not be difficult to see that the directional response (or directivity pattern as it is often called) of this transducer, when all the sections are joined together in the same phase, may be expressed as the product of two factors: (a) the directional response of the individual section:

$$\frac{\sin\left[(\pi d/\lambda)\sin\theta\right]}{(\pi d/\lambda)\sin\theta}$$

(b) the directional response of n point receivers spaced at a distance d apart:

$$\frac{\sin\left[(n\pi d/\lambda)\sin\theta\right]}{n\sin\left[(\pi d/\lambda)\sin\theta\right]}.$$

Here λ is the wavelength of the acoustic waves and θ is the direction of an incident wave relative to the line perpendicular to the array, or, in other words, the angle the wavefront makes with the array itself. The geometry of the system is shown in Fig. 34.

The two directional responses (a) and (b) are shown in Fig. 35, on a rectangular plot against sin θ, and it is clear

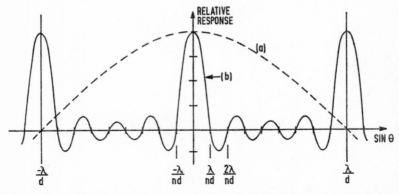

Fig. 35.—(a) The directional pattern of each individual section of the transducer; (b) the directional pattern of n point elements. ($n = 9$ in this example.)

that when the transducer sections are subject to no extra phase-shift, which is the condition for which the figure is drawn, there is no other main beam apart from the central one because at the values of θ where (b) has another main beam, the response (a) has a zero.

When phase-shifts are used to deflect (or scan) the beam, they compensate for the phase differences due to the difference of path lengths, $d\sin\theta$, between adjacent transducer elements.

Clearly this affects the pattern of response (b) due to the *n* spaced receivers and causes it to shift one way or the other along the sin θ scale; but it does not affect the pattern of response (a) at all, since this is fixed. Now response (a) effectively fixes the envelope of the curve along which the resultant peak response moves as the beam is deflected by phasing, so that as the deflection is increased, two things happen:

(i) the peak height of the resultant directional response diminishes, and

(ii) the adjacent "spurious main beam" of response (b), initially at an angle $\sin^{-1}(\lambda/d)$, ceases to be zero, but increases in magnitude according to response (a).

When the main peak has been deflected by an angle

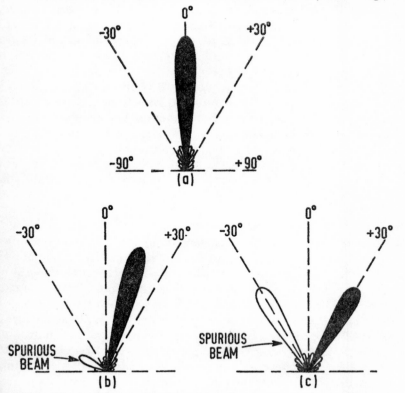

Fig. 36.—Showing how a spurious beam is introduced as the main beam is scanned electronically across a sector. This example is for $n = 9$ and $d = \lambda$.

$\sin^{-1}(\lambda/2d)$, its height has dropped approximately 3 dB and that of the "spurious main beam" has increased until it is now equal to the main peak. At greater deflections the spurious peak becomes virtually the main peak and the original main beam becomes only a spurious response. Thus it becomes clear that the limit of practicable deflection of the beam—or the half-width of the scanned sector—is at the value of $\theta = \sin^{-1}(\lambda/2d)$. At this point, the value of phase-shift which has been added between adjacent sections of the transducer is π radians or 180 degrees, so that alternate sections have been reversed in phase. This is another way of looking at the limit of the deflection system; a further change of 180 degrees per section merely restores everything to the initial position, since one cycle of a continuous wave is not distinguishable from another.

The position is shown in terms of a polar graph of beam response in Fig. 36, for a particular arrangement and length of transducer, namely $n = 9$ and $d = \lambda$. Here it is clear that the maximum width of scanned sector is 60 degrees and that ambiguous effects occur at the edges of this sector.

If a wider sector is required to be scanned there must be more sections (i.e. finer subdivision) in the transducer and in consequence more channels in the electronic equipment (and hence more expense!). If a finer beam is required, to give higher resolution within the sector, then the transducer must be longer. If the same sector is to be covered, this means still more sections in the transducer.

5.3 *Multiplicative signal processing*

It was stated in Section 3.1 that the high-resolution electronic-scanning sonar developed at the University of Bu. ningham was able to provide a very narrow beam in relation to the size of the transducer partly because it used "multiplicative signal processing". We must now take a closer look at this matter.

Basically the system is as shown in Fig. 37. The receiving transducer array, of length l, is divided into two halves as shown, so that the spacing of the centres of the two parts is $l/2$. Each part is connected separately to an electrical or electronic circuit which gives an output voltage at any instant proportional to the product of the two instantaneous voltages applied to it. If a signal wave arrives from the direction giving an angle

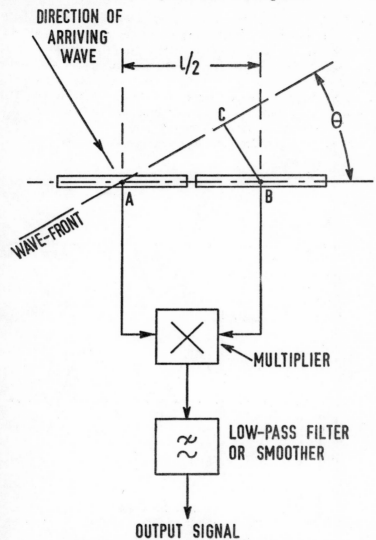

Fig. 37. The multiplicative signal processing system.

θ as shown, then we may take the wave at A as having the reference phase (i.e. zero) so that we may write it as $P \cos \omega t$, where ω is the angular frequency $(= 2\pi f$, where f is the frequency in cycles/sec) and t is time; we assume the acoustic pressure amplitude P is converted to a voltage amplitude V by the transducer without further phase shift, so that the electrical signal wave applied to the multiplier from A is $V \cos \omega t$. At B, the received wave has to travel an extra distance CB which is equal to $(l/2) \sin \theta$; thus the wave at B is delayed in phase by an angle $\theta_E = (\pi l/\lambda) \sin \theta$, where λ is the wavelength, giving the acoustic signal at B as $P \cos (\omega t - \theta_E)$ and the electrical signal as $V \cos (\omega t - \theta_E)$.

The result of multiplying together the two signals is illus-

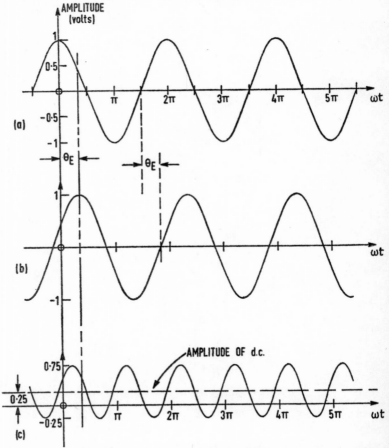

Fig. 38.—Showing the wave (c) produced by multiplying together the waves $\cos \omega t$ (in graph a) and $\cos (\omega t - \theta_E)$ in graph b), where $\theta_E = \pi/3$ radians or 60 degrees.

trated for the particular case of $\theta_E = \pi/3$ radians (or 60 degrees) and $V = 1$ volt in Fig. 38. The two received waves are shown at (a) and (b). For any particular point in time the amplitudes of the two waves are taken, multiplied together, and then this product plotted for the same point in time in graph (c). For example, at $t = 0$, curve (a) has a height of unity and curve (b) has a height of 0·5. The product is therefore 0·5 which is plotted for $t = 0$ in curve (c). It can be seen that when this is done for all points in time, the resultant graph (c) is a wave of double frequency (i.e. 2ω) but with its mean amplitude not zero as in the original waves (a) and (b), but at a level of 0·25 volt. If the double-frequency wave is smoothed away by passing the signal from the multiplier through a smoothing circuit (otherwise known as a low-pass filter) as shown in Fig. 37, then what is left is merely the direct-current component represented by the mean amplitude of 0·25 volt. Clearly if the signal wave had come from a different direction, the phase angle θ_E would have been different, and therefore the d.c. voltage would have been different. The d.c. voltage (for a constant acoustic wave amplitude) therefore varies with θ_E, being a maximum of 0·5 when $\theta_E = 0$ and a minimum of zero when $\theta_E = \pi/2$ radians (or 90 degrees). A graph of this variation forms the directional response of the multiplicative system, provided we also allow for the directional response of the two halves of the transducer in their own right.

We must now express this in simple mathematical form. Assuming the acoustic wave amplitude P is constant, then the voltage V from each half of the transducer will itself vary according to the angle θ because of the directional response of the transducer. If the transducer has uniform sensitivity along its length, then the directional response of each half is

$$\frac{\sin \left[(\pi l/2\lambda) \sin \theta \right]}{(\pi l/2\lambda) \sin \theta} \cdot$$

We can thus write the electrical signals at A and B as

$$V_0 \frac{\sin \left[(\pi l/2\lambda) \sin \theta \right]}{(\pi l/2\lambda) \sin \theta} \cos \omega t$$

and

$$V_0 \frac{\sin \left[(\pi l/2\lambda) \sin \theta \right]}{(\pi l/2\lambda) \sin \theta} \cos (\omega t + \theta_E)$$

respectively. When these are multiplied together we remember the trigonometric rule for the product of two cosines:

$$\cos \omega t \, . \, \cos (\omega t + \theta_E) = \tfrac{1}{2} \cos \theta_E + \tfrac{1}{2} \cos (2\omega t + \theta_E);$$

remembering also that the double-frequency component is smoothed out by the low-pass filter, and putting in the full expression for θ_E, we see that the final output signal is the d.c. component.

$$\tfrac{1}{2} V_0{}^2 \left\{ \frac{\sin \left[(\pi l/2\lambda) \sin \theta \right]}{(\pi l/2\lambda) \sin \theta} \right\}^2 \cos \left[(\pi l/\lambda) \sin \theta \right].$$

This then is the mathematical expression for the directional response of the system. It is shown as a function of $\sin \theta$ in Fig. 39. For comparison, the directional response of the same

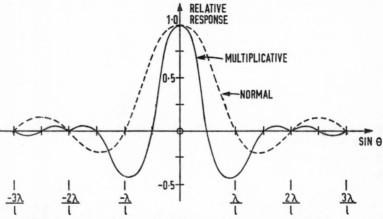

Fig. 39.—Comparison of the directional responses of multiplicative and normal systems.

transducer array used in the normal manner (i.e. with the outputs from the two halves merely connected together) is shown by dashed lines. It can be seen that the multiplicative system has only half the beamwidth.

It is very easy to work the multiplicative signal processing with the electronic-scanning sonar, as shown in the block-schematic diagram of Fig. 40, which may be compared with the receiving arrangements in the earlier diagram, Fig. 33. Individual delay lines (of half the length used in the non-multiplicative system) are used to scan the directional pattern of each half of the transducer (i.e. the term in braces in the last expression above), while an additional phase delay network is provided in one of the leads to the multiplier to scan the purely-multiplicative part of the directional pattern (i.e. the right-hand term in the last expression above).

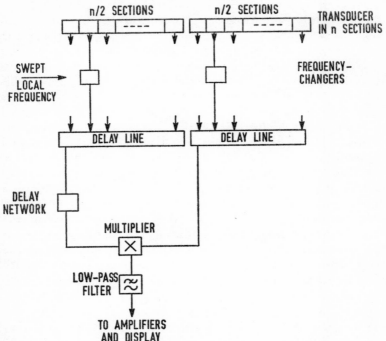

Fig. 40.—Schematic diagram of electronic-scanning receiver with multiplicative signal processing.

It must be observed that the low-pass filter following the multiplier must have its cut-off frequency sufficiently high to allow the pulsed signal to rise and decay fast enough to reproduce an adequate pulse shape. Its main requirement is to suppress the double frequency shown in Fig. 38, and this frequency will normally be at least 20 times the highest frequencies needed to pass the pulse.

It is an over-simplification to say that the halving of the beamwidth which this multiplicative system produces necessarily leads to a 2 : 1 improvement in the angular resolution,

i.e. in the closeness of angular spacing of two targets which are
at the same range and can yet be separately displayed by the
sonar. There are some quite complex factors involved in this
matter of angular resolution which have been dealt with in
research papers concerned with the effects in both sonar and
radar. But as far as sonar is concerned, used in the normal
manner from a ship-mounted platform, so that there is always
movement of the sonar relative to the targets during the
intervals between pulses, there is little doubt that when two
similar targets are observed over two or three pulses the
effective improvement in resolution really is about 2 : 1. This
is well demonstrated by some simple experimental results
shown in Fig. 41 (on page 72), obtained with the eight-channel
scanning sonar discussed in Section 3.2, operated in a harbour
basin at Plymouth. Here the beamwidth of the system used
normally, i.e. according to Fig. 33, was very close to 1·5 degrees.
We would thus expect to be able to separate clearly two small
targets spaced at about 3 degrees. The left-hand photograph
of the display shows that two small targets are just appearing
with distinct separation at 2·5 degrees spacing. When the
system was switched over to multiplicative working, the result
shown on the right was obtained; here the two targets are
quite distinct at a separation of 1·5 degrees. It will also be
seen that other objects in the harbour basin are better resolved.

A similar experiment carried out using the Birmingham high-
resolution system in Loch Ness gave similar results. An interesting result was obtained from this experiment when two very
small targets were carefully spaced one degree apart. The
multiplicative system successfully resolved them, but when the
equipment was changed over to the conventional "additive"
operation, resolution was not achieved.

It is clear that the multiplicative signal processing system is
very advantageous in practice.

5.4   *Signal-to-noise and signal-to-reverberation ratios in electronic-scanning sonars*

A reasonably adequate account of the nature of background
noise and of reverberation—whether from the sea-bottom, from
the sea surface, or from the various inhomogeneities in the
volume of the sea—was given in the author's companion book

"Underwater Observation Using Sonar". It was shown how these two factors limit the detection performance of sonar systems. Noise is generally regarded as that part of the undesired background, against which the target signal-echo has to be detected, which does not arise from the sonar's own transmission; reverberation is the general back-scatter of acoustic energy from the transmitted pulse. A general conclusion was that the signal-to-noise ratio, SNR, (which is obviously a measure of detectability of the signal echo) could be improved by raising the power level of the transmission; but the signal-to-reverberation ratio, SRR, (which is usually the dominant measure of detectability for nearly-horizontal beams in shallow water) could not be improved in this way since both signal and reverberation are equally dependent on the transmitted power level.

These conclusions lead us directly to the answer to the question: what effect does within-pulse electronic sector-scanning have on the SNR and SRR? In the scanning sonar the transmitted energy is spread over a wide sector of n times the angular width of the receiving beam. Thus the power level, or acoustic intensity at any given range, is only $1/n$ times that which would be obtained if all the power had been concentrated in a narrow beamwidth equal to the receiving beamwidth— as in a non-scanning sonar. The receiving noise level is, of course, not affected by scanning (at least, not in an ideal system), so that the SNR is worsened by $10 \log_{10} n$ decibels (i.e. if instead of using decibels, it is expressed as a power ratio, it is worsened by n times; if as a voltage ratio, by $\sqrt{(n)}$ times). However, the rate at which information is obtained (the "data rate") is increased by a ratio n, and this is not only some theoretical compensation for the loss of SNR which can be realized quite readily, but it also leads to a more graphic and interpretable display.

As regards the SRR, it can be seen that this is unchanged by scanning, since the change in power level per beamwidth affects signal and reverberation equally. The fact that the SNR is worsened by scanning, however, may mean that, whereas the SRR may have been the dominant factor in the non-scanning sonar because the noise level was well below the reverberation level, now the noise level may exceed the reverberation level so that the SRR is no longer the dominant factor. In these circumstances it would be wise design to increase the transmitted power so that the SRR once more became dominant. The advantage is clearly that as the SRR is not worsened by scanning, yet the data rate is increased by a ratio n, scanning gives a clear gain over non-scanning—quite apart from its operational convenience—if limitation by noise can be avoided.

6   Conclusions

It is thought that a good case has been made for the introduction of within-pulse electronic sector-scanning sonar into both fisheries research and fishing operations. Some further experimenting may be needed to establish the best parameters of the system for different applications. I am inclined to the view that while a system which has a scanned sector of say 50 or more beamwidths may well be needed and justified for research purposes, yet a scanned sector covering only say 16 or 20 beamwidths may be adequate for fish-finding, where the need for accurate and comprehensive portrayal of shape is less, while the need for cheapness is greater. The need to obtain a greater range of detection of single fish than any present design of electronic-scanning sonar can give is important; the range of detection is limited at present—as compared with a non-scanning sonar of the same beamwidth—by the fact that the transmitted power is spread out over a large number of beamwidths. But better methods of electronic processing of the received signal may restore this loss. The development of much cheaper electronic systems will also encourage the use of scanning. Present equipments, when available commercially, will cost several thousands of pounds each for the electronics; one may hope that this can eventually be reduced to say £1,000.

Further Reading for Chapter 2

Section 3

1 G. M. Voglis and J. C. Cook: "Underwater applications of an advanced acoustic scanning equipment", *Ultrasonics*, **4,** Jan. 1966, p. 1.

2 V. G. Welsby and J. R. Dunn: "A high-resolution electronic sector-scanning sonar," *J. Brit. Inst. Radio Engrs.*, **26,** Sept. 1963, p. 205.

3   V. G. Welsby, J. H. S. Blaxter and C. J. Chapman: "Electronically-scanned sonar in the investigation of fish behaviour", *Nature*, **199**, 1963, p. 980.

4   V. G. Welsby, J. R. Dunn, C. J. Chapman, D. P. Sharman and R. Priestley: "Further uses of electronically scanned sonar in the investigation of behaviour of fish", *Nature*, **203**, 1964, p. 588.

5   D. G. Tucker and V. G. Welsby: "Distinguishing moving targets on display photographs", *Proc. Symposium on Signal Processing, Inst. Electronic and Radio Engrs.*, 1964, Contribution No. 27A.

6   D. G. Tucker: "Electronic sector-scanning asdic", *J. Inst. Navigation*, **12**, 1959, p. 184.

7   D. G. Tucker and V. G. Welsby: "Electronic sector-scanning asdic: An improved fish-locator and navigational instrument", *Nature*, **185**, 1960, p. 277.

8   D. G. Tucker, V. G. Welsby, L. Kay, M. J. Tucker, A. R. Stubbs, and J. G. Henderson: "Underwater echo-ranging with electronic sector-scanning: Sea trials on R.R.S. *Discovery II*", *J. Brit. Inst. Radio Engrs.*, **19**, 1959, p. 681.

9   D. G. Tucker: "Directional echo-sounding", *Int. Hydrographic Review*, **37**, 1960, p. 43.

10   E. A. Howson and J. R. Dunn: "Directional echo-sounding", *J. Inst. Navigation*, **14**, 1961, p. 348.

Section 4

11   D. G. Tucker and V. G. Welsby: "Sector-scanning sonar for fisheries purposes", *Modern Fishing Gear of the World* 2, 1964, p. 367.

12   ' "Sector-scanning" may be sonar of the future', *World Fishing*, **12**, Sept. 1963, p. 48.

Section 5

13   D. G. Tucker, V. G. Welsby and R. Kendell: "Electronic sector-scanning", *J. Brit. Inst. Radio Engrs.*, **18**, 1958, p. 465.

14   B. S. McCartney: "An improved electronic sector-scanning sonar receiver", *J. Brit. Inst. Radio Engrs.*, **22**, 1961, p. 481.

15   D. G. Tucker: "The signal/noise performance of electro-acoustic strip arrays", *Acustica*, **8**, 1958, p. 53 (Discusses multiplicative signal processing).

16   V. G. Welsby and D. G. Tucker: "Multiplicative receiving arrays", *J. Brit. Inst. Radio Engrs.*, **19**, 1959, p. 369.

17   V. G. Welsby: Multiplicative receiving arrays; the angular resolution of targets in a sonar system with electronic scanning", *J. Brit. Inst. Radio Engrs.*, **22,** 1961, p. 5.

18   D. G. Tucker: "Multiplicative arrays in radio-astronomy and sonar systems", *J. Brit. Inst. Radio Engrs.*, **25,** 1963, p. 113.

19   V. G. Welsby: "The angular resolution of a receiving aperture in the absence of noise", *J. Brit. Inst. Radio Engrs.*, **26,** 1963, p. 115.

20   E. Shaw and D. E. N. Davies: "Theoretical and experimental studies of the resolution performance of multiplicative and additive aerial arrays", *J. Inst. Electronic and Radio Engrs.*, **28,** 1964, p. 279.

21   J. J. Faran and R. Hills: "The Application of Correlation Techniques to Acoustic Receiving Systems", Harvard University, Acoustic Research Labs, Tech. Memo. No. 28, 1952.

22   A. Berman and C. S. Clay: "Theory of time-averaged product arrays", *J. Acoustical Soc. America*, **29,** 1957, p. 806.

23   A. A. Ksienski: "Multiplicative processing antennas for radar applications", *J. Inst. Electronic and Radio Engrs.*, **29,** 1965, p. 53.

24   R. Blommendaal: "A note on multiplicative receiving systems for radar", *J. Inst. Electronic and Radio Engrs.*, **28,** 1964, p. 317.

25   H. V. Cottony and A. C. Wilson: "A High Resolution Rapid Scan Antenna", National Bureau of Standards, Report No. 6723, 1960. (This paper describes a system of electronic-scanning which can be applied to sonar and is, indeed, similar to that believed to be used in the Admiralty Research Laboratory's scanning sonar.)

Chapter 3

A Forward Look

1 Introduction

In Chapter 1 we surveyed the present state of sonar in fisheries and noted some of its deficiencies. In Chapter 2 we considered a new development in sonar for fisheries which, while not yet available commercially, passed out of the engineering research stage some years ago and has already been developed for commercial manufacture. In the present chapter it is proposed to describe briefly some new possibilities in sonar for fisheries which are still in the engineering research stage but look very promising. As none of them has, at the time of writing, been subjected to an operational trial—they are not yet advanced enough for that—it is possible that none of them will prove operationally successful, and that by the time this book is five years old they will have been forgotten. It is more probable, however, that at least one of the schemes will prove successful and be by then in an advanced state of development. This is a risk in all research.

Three proposed new types of system will be described; they are all part of the sonar research programme at the University of Birmingham. They are:

(a) Wideband sonar systems
(b) Systems exploiting non-linear acoustic wave interactions
(c) Digital sonar systems.

Other types of system are possible, of course, and some of them are the subject of research elsewhere (e.g. at the National Institute of Oceanography, and at various commercial firms, as well as at Birmingham). It is worth while to list some of them:

(i) other kinds of digital or hard-limited sonar systems,
(ii) high-power low-frequency systems (e.g. working at 7·5

97

kc/s with perhaps some hundreds of kilowatts of acoustic
power and a range of many kilometres)

(iii) very-low-frequency systems (e.g. working around 100
c/s)

(iv) high-frequency image-forming systems, using an acoustic lens or mirror with acoustic/electronic image
convertor

(v) continuous-wave doppler-detection systems

(vi) frequency-modulation systems

(vii) system using within-pulse electronic scanning of a pencil
beam on two axes.

These do not necessarily all have promise for fisheries applications. It should be mentioned, too, that much other research
goes on connected with the propagation of acoustic waves in
the sea, with the sonar-target characteristics of fish and other
organisms, with the reverberation characteristics of the sea-
floor, with improved signal-processing methods, with the
fundamentals of visual and aural displays, etc. This cannot be
discussed further here.

2   Wideband sonar

There has been for over a decade a little experimental evidence
that the target strength of fish depends on frequency and that
the way in which it varies with frequency may be characteristic
of the size and/or species of the fish. It thus appeared to the
author many years ago that there would be important applications for a sonar system which covered a very wide band of
frequency (e.g. a ten-to-one ratio of upper to lower frequency),
so that, in addition to the usual display of range and bearing,
the way in which a particular target varied with frequency
could also be displayed. It seemed that such an equipment
would be invaluable in fisheries research and might also be
useful in fish catching to enable the species and size of fish to be
determined before catching. Consequently research was started
towards the development of such a system. The problems were
formidable, however, and the last of them has only very
recently been solved. The most basic of the problems are those
concerned with getting transducers which can operate over the
wide frequency-band and also give a constant beamwidth over

this band. It is clearly of no value if the beamwidth varies with frequency, since then the apparent frequency response of a target would depend on whereabouts in the beam it lay. Yet the beamwidth of an ordinary transducer, being determined by the number of wavelengths in the length of the transducer, does depend on frequency; it is, in fact, more-or-less inversely proportional to frequency. So the research effort at Birmingham was concentrated on the transducer problem. But before we discuss this work further, we need to look at the evidence now available on the matter of the target strength of fish, on which topic research has been proceeding elsewhere, notably at the Fisheries Laboratory at Lowestoft and at Kelvin Hughes.

2.1 *Fish target strength as a function of size and frequency*

It has become clear that the target strength of a fish is a very complex matter and a great deal more work has to be done before it can be claimed that it is understood. But certain broad principles can be discussed.

Experimental measurements made by the two establishments already named have related the target strength of fish (as seen from above, i.e. in dorsal aspect) to their length, at a fixed frequency of 30 kc/s. The measured values all lie within the hatched area on the graph in Fig. 42, and indeed the best-fitting straight line relating target strength to length has the same slope as the limit lines shown, i.e. about 9 dB increase in target strength for a doubling of length. This may be interpreted as indicating that the equivalent spherical target of reflecting material has a cross-section *area* proportional to the cube of the fish length, i.e. presumably proportional to the *volume* of the fish. It is thought that for the side aspect of the fish, the target strength rises even more rapidly with length. (It should be remembered that these target strengths are expressed in decibels relative to a sphere of 2 m radius.)

There is still very little direct experimental data on the variation of target strength with frequency. As a result of experiments with scale models and of theoretical analysis, Dr. Haslett of Kelvin Hughes suggests that the relationship of target strength to frequency depends on size roughly in the manner shown in Fig. 43, where the author has taken the liberty of simplifying Haslett's curves. There is at low frequencies a range where the fish is small compared with the wavelength of the sonar signal, and in this region theory suggests a *very* steep dependence of target strength on frequency. At much higher frequencies where the fish dimensions are large compared with the wavelength, the dependence is much less, but still consider-

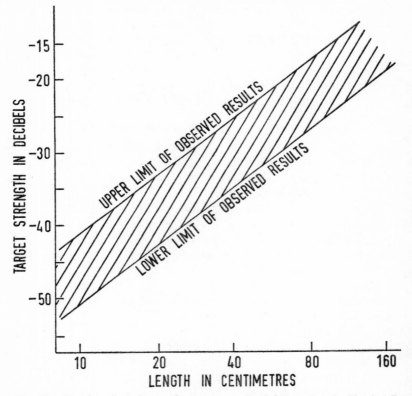

Fig. 42.—Showing dependence of target strength of fish on length. Nearly all observed results lay within the hatched area.
Frequency 30 kc/s. Dorsal aspect of fish. Cod, herring, perch, plaice were used.

able. In between these regions the target strength has theoretically a very complicated and oscillating dependence on frequency, but as experimental support for this is practically non-existent, only a simplified dashed curve has been drawn in the graph. It can be seen that the experimental data of Fig. 42 is at least not too inconsistent with these curves, as can be seen by the intercepts of the curve on the 30 kc/s ordinate. It must be accepted that unless the theory and laboratory work are very much in error, there should be a steep dependence of target

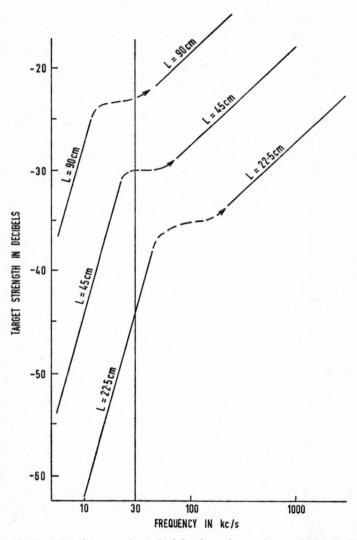

Fig. 43.—Showing the general trend of the dependence of target strength of fish in dorsal aspect on frequency. L = length of fish.

strength on frequency and that the actual shape of a wideband frequency response should give a lot of information about the size of the fish.

Because of the factors discussed above, the research work on wideband sonar has been directed mainly towards obtaining wideband operation over the frequency range 5–100 kc/s. But there is also a possibility that examination of the frequency response of fish echoes in a much lower frequency range, e.g. 200 c/s–2 kc/s, may be worth while since swim-bladder resonances probably occur in this region; and discovery of the resonant frequency, in conjunction with the other information discussed above, may well help to identify the fish species. Information on this matter is also very scarce, although some work has been done on it at the National Institute of Oceanography. Evidently the prime need is for a wideband sonar as a research tool in the first instance, so that information on the frequency response of fish as sonar targets may be obtained.

2.2 *Wideband receiving transducer*

Reverting to the problem of making transducers which give a constant beamwidth over a wide band of frequency, we have to realize that in their normal use transducers

(a) have a beamwidth which is approximately inversely proportional to the frequency, and

(b) have a response of sensitivity with frequency which shows a very marked resonance at a particular frequency.

For wideband use, therefore, we have to find a way of overcoming these two difficulties.

The requirements on transmission and reception are not the same. Although it is desirable to have the same constant beamwidth on both transmission and reception, it is not essential, and the bearing accuracy of the wideband sonar system can, if it proves necessary, be allowed to depend mainly on say the receiving transducer. More fundamental is the fact that sonar detection is usually limited, not by the noise arising in the receiver itself, but by the noise arising in the sea which is of higher level except at frequencies above 100 kc/s. This means that, within limits, the efficiency of the receiving transducer is not of primary importance, since the signal-to-noise ratio is determined by the transmitted acoustic power level relative to the sea noise and is largely independent of the ratio of signal level to the noise generated (e.g. by thermal motion of electrons) in the receiver itself. Over the limits within which this statement applies, we can afford to use receiving transducer elements which have their resonance right outside the frequency band of the sonar. The variation of sensitivity with frequency can then be relatively small, although the sensitivity is itself lower

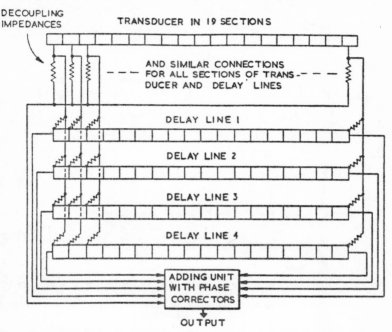

Fig. 44.—Schematic arrangement of wideband array system using line transducer and delay circuits.

than usual. This is not so acceptable at the transmitter, since detection is controlled by the acoustic power level transmitted.

To obtain a beamwidth which is reasonably constant over the frequency band, the author originally put forward a scheme whereby the beamwidth in one axis was maintained reasonably narrow and constant, but in the other axis the response was nearly omnidirectional. A line transducer was used, as shown in Fig. 44, divided into sections and connected to a series of delay lines (or phase-shifting circuits). Each of the latter has a phase-shift which increases with frequency, so that at each end the signals correspond to an effective directional pattern which is deflected by an amount which increases with frequency but at the same time becomes narrower due to the increasing number of wavelengths in the length of the transducer. Successive delay lines have a successively larger range of phase-shifts. Then, with phase corrections to ensure that the outputs from the various delay lines are in phase at all frequencies, the outputs are added together.

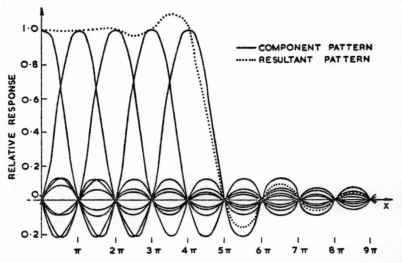

Fig. 45.—Component patterns and resultant pattern at upper frequency limit of the system shown in Fig. 44.

Now at the lowest frequency the phase-shifts are very small and the various directional patterns are deflected by only a very small proportion of their beamwidth; thus the resultant directional pattern is almost the same as that due to the transducer itself. But as the frequency rises and the patterns narrow, they become relatively more spread out in direction, so that compensation is obtained. At the upper frequency limit they are as shown in Fig. 45, where the angular scale is strictly defined by $x = (\pi l/\lambda) \sin \theta$, where l is the length of the transducer and λ is the wavelength, θ being the signal direction relative to the normal axis of the transducer. But if the beam is fairly narrow

Fig. 48.—Twisted, or hyperbolic paraboloidal array. (This is a wooden model, where the straight strips represent line transducers.)

Fig. 50—Actual receiving transducer mounted in its frame for experimental tests. Beamwidth approximately constant over range 8—80 kc/s.

Fig. 51.—Experimental wideband transmitting transducer mounted in frame. The transducer elements are the rings forming the tapered structure at the bottom of the picture. The electrical networks are in the canister above.

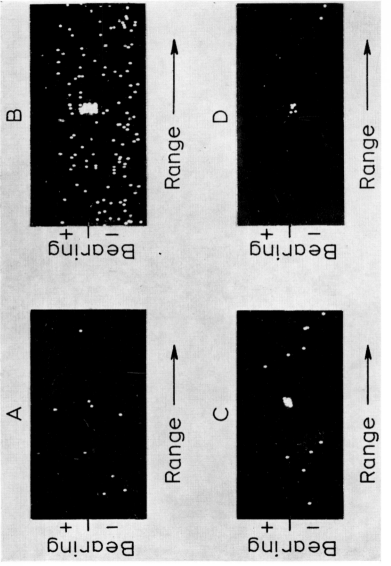

Fig. 57.—Results of laboratory tests on digital sonar system, using a "synthetic target" signal and background noise. (a) display from a single transmission with a high threshold setting; signal power equal to noise power. (b) as in (a) but with [...] times (a) as in (a) but signal power three times noise power, (d) as in (b) but with low threshold setting.

(20 degrees was used in the experimental work) then the x-scale may be taken to be proportional to θ, and for 20 degrees beam-width the angle corresponding to $x = \pi$ is about 2·5 degrees.

It can be seen that this system tends to keep the overall beam-

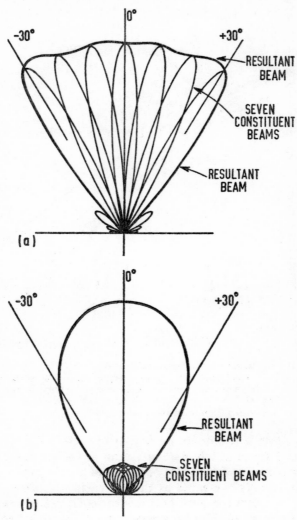

Fig. 46.—Showing principle of constant-beamwidth array (a) at frequency 6ω, (b) at frequency ω.

width constant. This is shown rather more clearly in the polar
graphs of Fig. 46, where the case considered is one with seven
constituent beams and a 60-degree beamwidth, with an
operating frequency range from frequency ω to frequency 6ω.
At ω, the constituent beams largely coincide, but at 6ω they
overlap only at approximately their 3-dB points; thus at ω the

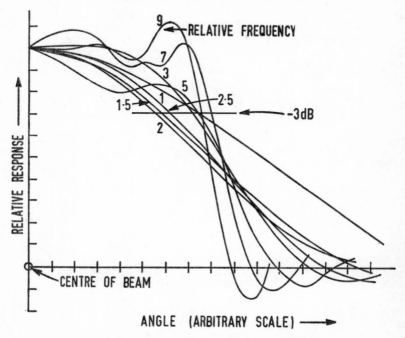

Fig. 47.—Directional responses of wideband receiver over the 9:1 frequency range
are shown for one half of the beam. The response corresponding to frequency ω is
marked 1, that for frequency 9ω is marked 9, and correspondingly for intermediate
frequencies. The relative response is shown on a voltage scale; the -3dB level
occurs for a relative voltage response of 0·71.

peak response is five or six times that of each individual beam
(the sensitivity of which is smaller than at 6ω because of being
spread out over a wider angle) whereas at 6ω the peak response
is approximately the same as that of each constituent beam.
Clearly, although the 3-dB beamwidth remains fairly constant,
the actual shape of the beam varies somewhat with frequency.
For the array as shown in Fig. 44, with a nominal 3-dB beam-

width of 20 degrees, the beam patterns, plotted on rectangular axes, vary with frequency as shown in Fig. 47. It seems at present that this is the best result achievable. The system was tested experimentally for a frequency band 9–81 kc/s, and the results agreed with the theory very closely. The 3-dB beamwidth varies only $\pm 9\%$ over the frequency range.

In working on the above system, Dr. J. C. Morris got the idea that, instead of using delay lines to produce deflected patterns from a single line transducer, a series of line transducers physically mounted at different angles would produce just the same result. Moreover, he saw that if they were mounted at such transverse spacings as to build up a square array then a constant narrow beamwidth could be obtained on all axes and not just the one axis of the previous system. The array then became a hyperbolic paraboloidal surface, as shown in a model in Fig. 48 (third art section, page 105). This new system has a number of advantages over the previous one:

(a) it gives a constant-width roughly-conical beam
(b) it requires no complex electrical networks
(c) it can be effective over a very wide bandwidth by either
    (i) using a large number of very narrow line transducers,
    or (ii) using a twisted continuous transducer surface.

Beamshapes calculated for this array at the lowest working frequency (ω) and at 20 times this frequency are shown in Fig. 49. These are plotted as three-dimensional graphs with rectangular axes of angle θ and ϕ, scaled in degrees. The intersections of the normal planes through these axes with the surface of the graph are shown by heavy lines. The 3-dB response is also shown by heavy lines, and it can be seen that at ω the 3-dB cross-section is almost circular, whereas at 20ω it is almost square. But apart from such changes, and also those corresponding to Fig. 47, the beam is remarkably constant.

A working transducer has been made on this basis, using strips of lead zirconate-titanate as the active elements, operating below resonance. It is shown in Fig. 50 (page 106), and works over the frequency range 8–80 kc/s approximately with a 20-degree beamwidth. This is intended as the receiver of an operational wideband sonar equipment. Tests have shown its performance to agree satisfactorily with predictions.

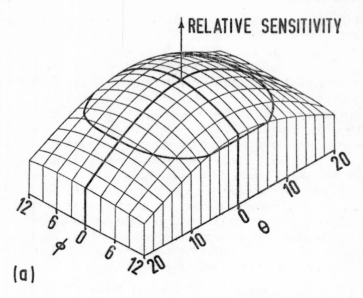

(a)

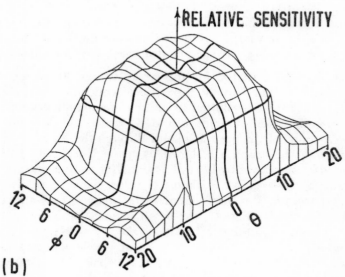

(b)

Fig. 49.—Beamshapes of the hyperbolic-paraboloidal array: (a) at the lowest frequency ω, (b) at 20ω.

2.3 *Wideband transmitting transducer*

It has already been mentioned that the problem of the transmitting transducer is more severe in that reasonable efficiency is necessary in order to obtain a signal intensity above the noise intensity at the end of the transmission path. The use of a transducer in a frequency range well removed from resonance is therefore not attractive for transmitting, acceptable though it may be for reception. The basis on which an efficient transmitter covering a wide frequency band was designed was therefore this: a series of resonant ring-type transducer elements was mounted on a common axis, with resonant frequencies (and therefore sizes) forming a tapered sequence. The spacing of resonant frequencies between adjacent elements was such that the frequencies at which the response was 3 dB below the peak coincided. Electrical networks were used to ensure that at these 3-dB points the outputs from the two contributing transducers were in phase for signals received along the axis. In this way the whole 9 : 1 frequency range could be covered with 23 elements (each with a Q-factor of about 6) and with a reasonably smooth response over the band. Directivity would then be assured by the use of an exponential reflecting horn around the transducer array. This transducer has been partly made and is shown (without the horn) in Fig. 51 (page 107). At the time of writing it still awaits test and calibration. This model operates from 20 to 100 kc/s with 17 elements.

While it is likely that this transducer will meet the requirement of the wide-band sonar, it now seems very probable that an alternative wide-band transmitter can be made using non-linear acoustic wave interactions which will be described in the next Section. It may well be that this will prove a better method. In any case, it should soon be possible to assemble the whole wide-band sonar for trials.

3 The exploitation of non-linearity in underwater acoustics

We have seen that while highly-directive low-frequency and wideband sonar systems have very attractive operational features and offer the possibility of a considerable extension in the range of information obtainable by sonar, their realization in practice is hampered by the difficulty of obtaining suitable transducers. A solution to this difficulty may well be the use of non-linear wave interactions in a new class of transmitting and receiving devices.

Non-linearity in acoustics is not new; in various forms it has been recognized and studied theoretically and practically for a long time. For instance, it arises in the propagation of explosive waves, in cavitation, etc. But the deliberate exploitation of non-linearity to obtain desirable effects otherwise difficult or impossible to achieve is relatively new, and the work being done at the University of Birmingham by the author's colleagues, especially Dr. H. O. Berktay, to develop new sonar techniques using non-linearity is a significant proportion of all the work on this subject.

3.1   *The nature of acoustic non-linearity*

What do we mean by linearity and non-linearity? In mathematical terms, we find that in the development of the basic theory of acoustic wave propagation there are normally (i.e. in the usual text-books) certain simplifications made during the course of the analysis which amount, in effect, to the assumptions that

(a) the density of the medium, represented by ρ (the Greek letter "rho"), is unaffected by the compressional and dilatational effects of the acoustic wave, and

(b) the compressibility of the medium (i.e. the change in volume produced by unit applied pressure) is also unaffected by the magnitude of the acoustic disturbance. Compressibility is the reciprocal of the "bulk modulus" κ (Greek "kappa"). That the first of these cannot be strictly true is quite obvious, since if the pressure is increased, the medium is compressed and its density must increase—even if only by a very small amount. The popular statement that "water is incompressible", while obviously untrue, is a simple illustration of the fact that in a liquid the effect is very small. It is less obvious that the compressibility is not constant, and again the effect is small. Thus, provided the acoustic intensities involved are not very large, it is not unreasonable to make these two assumptions since they lead to a very great simplification in the mathematical work. The system, with these assumptions, becomes a linear one, since the response of any part of the system is linearly proportional to the applied excitation. If two or more waves exist in the medium, at different frequencies, they do not interact at all; all responses are merely the sum of the effects of the two or more waves taken separately, and no new frequencies are introduced. The velocity of propagation is $\sqrt{(\kappa/\rho)}$, and so, with these assumptions, is a constant for all acoustic disturbances in the medium.

If the assumptions are not made, so that both ρ and κ have values dependent on the instantaneous acoustic pressures, then, as we have said, the mathematics become very complicated. If two or more waves exist, they interact and the total effect at any point in the medium is no longer the sum of the effects of each wave taken separately; moreover, new waves at new frequencies are introduced. The system is now non-linear, since most responses are *not* linearly proportional to the excitations. If the wave amplitudes are small, the non-linearity is small, and the usual neglect of it is reasonably justified. But if the wave amplitudes are made large, the non-linear effects become very significant.

It is fairly easy to demonstrate the effects of non-linearity without the use of mathematics by noticing that the abandonment of the assumptions that ρ and κ are constant means that no longer is the velocity of propagation, $\sqrt{(\kappa/\rho)}$, a constant. It now has a different value for different values of the pressure in the medium. In other words, different parts of an applied waveform travel with different speeds. The distortion this produces is easily visualized, using the graphical technique of Fig. 52.

We suppose that a sinusoidal time-waveform is generated at some point in the medium by a planar transducer of relatively large size as measured in wavelengths. This waveform is shown at (b) in the figure. The wave thus generated propagates through the medium as a plane wave (owing to the large size of the transducer) without spreading. We may also assume for the present purpose that there is no energy absorption. But owing to the variation of density and compressibility with acoustic pressure, the velocity of propagation is different for different amplitudes of pressure. For simplicity let us assume that the velocity is given by its nominal value plus (or minus) a

small amount which is roughly proportional to the instantaneous acoustic pressure amplitude (positive or negative).
Then at a point of observation at some distance from the transducer there will be a different arrival time for the different

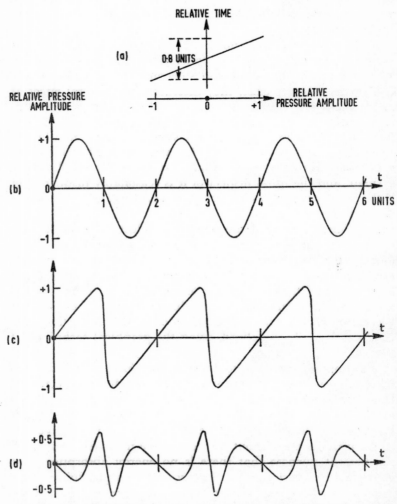

Fig. 52.—Showing distortion due to non-linear propagation. (a) Graph of arrival
time against amplitude at point of observation, (b) source waveform, (c) waveform
at point of observation, (d) difference waveform between (b) and (c).

amplitudes, as shown at (a) in Fig. 52, where the unit of time is quite arbitrary as this is only an illustrative example.

We now notice that, with our assumptions, the wave at the point of observation will have the same peak amplitude as that of the source, but that any small increment at a particular point on the waveform will have been subject to the time delay corresponding to curve (a). For example, an increment of pressure around the amplitude $+ 0.5$ has been subject to a delay of 0.2 units of time less than the delay for an increment around zero amplitude; and the peak has been delayed by 0.4 units less. Allowing for this, the time-waveform at the point of observation is easily drawn, as shown at (c). This is clearly a very distorted wave, and is no longer sinusoidal. Those familiar with observing waveforms in electronic apparatus will immediately recognize this waveform as one containing numerous harmonic frequencies, i.e. if the original frequency is f, then the wave now contains also $2f$, $3f$, $4f$, etc. This is readily demonstrated by subtracting the original wave (b) from the distorted wave (c), thus obtaining the waveform of the distortion components as shown in (d). There is a very obvious $2f$ component visible by inspection.

A more complicated, but much more important case is demonstrated in Fig. 53. Here we assume that two different frequencies are applied to the transducer, so that the source waveform is the sum of the wave of the frequency which we may call $3f$, shown at (a), and the wave of frequency $2f$ shown at (b). Thus waveform (c), which is merely (a) and (b) added together, represents the wave at the source. At the same point of observation as before (so that the time graph at (a) in Fig. 52 still applies), this wave becomes as shown at (d). Again, this is clearly distorted, and the nature of the distortion can be observed more clearly by subtracting the source waveform (c) from the distorted waveform (d), the result being shown at (e). Now it is not quite so easy to see the constitution of this wave by inspection as it was with the simpler case of Fig. 52, but the process of seeing it is greatly aided by the graphs of small waves of frequency $5f$ and f shown at (f) and (g) respectively. It is readily apparent that $5f$ is contained in the distortion wave; the sharp peaks at $t=1$ and $t=5$ also correspond to a content of f. Quite clearly the distortion due to non-linear propagation has

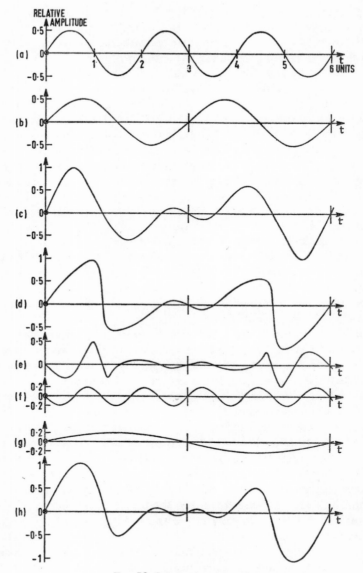

Fig. 53. See caption page 119.

introduced, among other products, the sum frequency of the two applied waves (i.e. $3f + 2f = 5f$) and the difference frequency (i.e. $3f - 2f = f$). Just as confirmation, if we add waves (f) and (g) to the source wave (c) we obtain wave (h); while this is not quite the same as the true distorted wave (d), it clearly has many of its characteristics, in particular the steepened slopes at around $t = 1.2$ and $t = 4.8$.

To those familiar with electronic circuits, in which non-linearity may be exploited for useful ends (as well as being an unmitigated nuisance, as in sound reproducers) it may seem that this effect is the same as that which occurs when two tones are applied to a non-linear circuit. So it is, up to a point. Since it is the elastic (or energy-storing) parameters of the acoustic medium which vary with pressure, and not the dissipative (or energy-absorbing) parameters—which we have assumed to be absent anyway in our example—it is clearly to non-linear capacitance or inductance and not to non-linear resistance that the acoustic non-linearity corresponds. But the acoustic effect is distributed all along the path of propagation, and in the non-spreading plane-wave example above the nearest electronic or electrical analogy is a non-linear loss-free transmission line. The travelling-wave parametric amplifier is an example.

3.2   *The proposed uses of acoustic non-linearity*

It will be clear from the account given above that the distortion of the wave increases as it propagates through the medium, and thus the amplitude of the difference-frequency wave which is generated increases; so also does that of the sum-frequency

---

Fig. 53.—Showing the production of sum and difference frequencies due to non-linear propagation.

The graph of time against amplitude for the point of observation is the same as for the previous figure. (a) One source waveform of frequency $3f$, (b) the other source waveform of frequency $2f$, (c) resultant source waveform, i.e. linear addition of (a) and (b), (d) distorted waveform at point of observation, (e) difference waveform between (c) and (d), (f) wave of frequency $5f$, relative amplitude (peak) 0·2, (g) wave of frequency f (i.e. difference frequency), relative amplitude (peak) 0·2, (h) result of adding (f) plus (g) to the source waveform (c). While this is not exactly like waveform (d), it is clearly approaching it, notably in the steepening of the slope just after $t = 1$ unit and just before $t = 5$ units.

wave, but we are not at present concerned with this. Naturally, the ideal conditions we have postulated will never apply exactly in practice; it is not possible to keep the wave entirely plane, to confine the flow of energy to a parallel-sided tube, nor to avoid absorption losses in the medium. These departures from the ideal, together with others which will apply in the open conditions of the sea, e.g. turbulence and inhomogeneities of various kinds, will mean that the amplitude of the source wave will decrease as it propagates and thus the rate of increase of distortion will diminish. Beyond a certain distance from the source there will be no further growth in the amplitude of the difference-frequency wave, and it will then start to decrease.

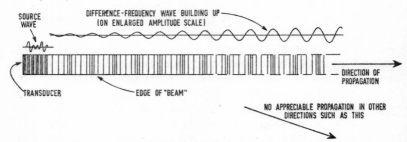

Fig. 54.—Showing the directional nature of the difference-frequency wave propagation.

The situation is thus roughly as shown in Fig. 54. The transducer generates plane waves which are indicated by the lines parallel to the transducer, showing very diagramatically the regions of increased hydrostatic pressure, due to the acoustic pressure, where the lines are close, and the regions of reduced pressure due to the negative acoustic half-cycles of pressure where the lines are more widely spaced. The complex waveform of the spatial wave, containing two frequencies, is also shown just above the beam. Over some distance the energy remains confined to the parallel-sided beam indicated by the full lines at right angles to the transducer, and due to the non-linear action or distortion the difference-frequency wave is generated at ever-increasing amplitude along this beam. This has been indicated diagrammatically both by the parallel-line system (with which it is hard to show relative amplitudes) and by a spatial waveform graph above the beam. Of course, the source wave is also present along the beam, and at much larger amplitude than the difference-frequency wave, but this has not been continued in the diagram after the first few cycles since it would obscure everything else. After a certain distance the parallel-sided beam begins to be less well-formed and energy begins to diverge, and this is indicated in the diagram by marking the beam edges with dashed lines instead of full lines. The difference-frequency wave then increases less rapidly.

What it is hoped is now clear is that the difference-frequency wave is propagated on a highly-directional basis. Along directions other than that of the original beam there is little energy propagated. Its directivity is indeed practically the same as that of the original source wave. The significance of this is considerable. Although in the graphical example we took the source frequencies as $3f$ and $2f$, giving a difference-frequency of f, there is no reason why the source frequencies should not be say $100f$ and $99f$, giving a difference-frequency of about one-hundredth of the source frequencies. The size of the transducer was chosen to be large enough in wavelengths, at $100f$, to give a narrow beam; but at a frequency of f it would have negligible directivity. Yet here we have a wave of frequency f generated with the full directivity of $100f$! This is clearly a matter of very great practical potentiality.

Another way of looking at this matter which is the basis of the existing mathematical treatments is to consider that all along the high-frequency beam the non-linear interaction is generating tiny sources of the difference frequency, and that these form a very long "end-fire" array. An end-fire array is one (well-known in radio work, but rather unusual in acoustics) which forms a beam with its axis in line with the array, and not at right angles as in the usual "broadside" arrays. This end-fire array is long in wavelengths even at the low difference-frequency; hence its high directivity.

It is possible, using explosive sources, to generate wave distortion as great as—or even greater than—that shown in Figs. 52 and 53. But with sinusoidal generators and normal transducers the amplitudes which can be obtained do not give anything like such great distortion, and the diagrams must be regarded as exaggerated merely for explanatory purposes. The intensity of the difference-frequency wave is actually bound to be very small compared with that of the source waves, and this is the price which has to be paid for an otherwise attractive system. But it is quite possible to have the intensity at a distant point as great as that which would be obtained if the same power were applied to a transducer of the same size directly at the low frequency. This arises because in the latter case there would be no directionality and the applied power would be radiated in all directions; whereas in the non-linear case what power is available at the low frequency is concentrated in a very narrow beam. And, of course, the directionality is usually very important in its own right. So here the non-linear system gives a clear operational gain.

Another way of regarding this is that if the directionality is essential anyway, then to obtain it directly in the usual way would require a huge transducer. To have to mount a transducer say 10 m in diameter and weighing many tons would be a high price to pay for saving the few kilowatts of power which would be needed to give the same effect using non-linearity and a transducer measured only in centimetres.

Another important matter to notice is that, as we have had cause to mention in earlier discussions, most electro-acoustic transducers are unable to transmit effectively a band of frequencies wider than about one-fifth of the centre frequency of the band. It is therefore not possible either to use very short pulses or to vary the frequency over a wide range. But in the non-linear system just described, the difference-frequency can be varied over say a 10 : 1 range by merely varying one of the source frequencies by say 10% (assuming they are as high as 100 times the difference-frequency). The transmitting transducer can certainly tolerate this 10% variation, and so we have a *really* wideband transmitting system, with constant beamwidth over the frequency band if the parameters are suitably chosen.

It can also be seen that if the high-frequency transducer is divided into sections, and each one is connected electrically via phase-shifters, then the beam may be deflected from its normal position. In consequence, the difference-frequency beam is also deflected by the same amount. Thus deflection of the very directive low-frequency beam may be effected merely by phasing the high-frequency transducer.

These various features of non-linear beam production open up the door to some new kinds of sonar system which have hitherto been impracticable. Some examples are listed below.

(i) A fish-finding sonar operating in the frequency band 7–30 kc/s, with a range of 2 km on a single cod, angular resolution of 2 degrees, range resolution of 25 cm, using peak power of 50 kW with mean power well under 1 kW; transducer only 35 cm long.

(ii) A sonar system having a bandwidth covering a 10 : 1 ratio of frequencies and thus able to display the frequency response as well as range and bearing of the targets.

(iii) A highly-directive very low frequency system operating, for example, over the range 500 to 2,000 c/s with constant beamwidth; this should be able to detect the resonances of the swim-bladders of fish. It could also have great possibilities for the communication of information underwater over long ranges.

Another interesting example of what seems possible using non-linear acoustics is this. Suppose we specify a sonar system for fish-detection which is to have a 1-degree resolution and a transducer not exceeding 50 cm in length, and is to give a detection range of 460 m on a single cod. Then using a conventional system, we need to operate at 150 kc/s in order to get the beam required with the specified length of transducer. The losses in sea-water are such that the transmitted power would need to exceed 2 kW during the pulse. However, using a non-linear system with source frequencies of 175 and 125 kc/s (this would need a transducer with alternate elements resonant at each frequency) so that the actual sonar frequency was 50 kc/s, the total transmitted power would have to be only about 0·7 kW at the source frequencies, i.e. *less* than in the normal case. This rather surprising result comes about because of the fact that the losses in the water are roughly 100 times as great (over the distance concerned) at 150 kc/s as at 50 kc/s, and the efficiency of non-linear generation, although low, is still sufficient to compensate for this.

To what extent are these proposals justified and supported

by experimental evidence? So far no complete sonar system has
been built using these principles. But Dr. Berktay and his team
at Birmingham have experimental confirmation of most of the
fundamental matters. As an example, we can give his experimental results for the constancy of beamwidth over a 10 : 1
frequency range; these are shown in Fig. 55, from which it can
be seen that a constancy of better than ± 1 degree was

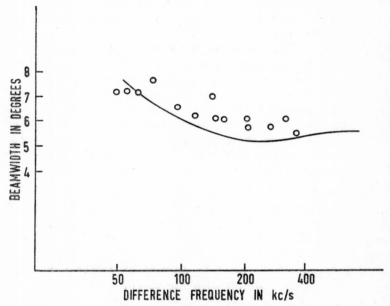

Fig. 55.—Showing experimental results of constant-beamwidth non-linear
transmitter. The circles indicate experimental measurements, and the line shows
the theoretical prediction. (*After H. O. Berktay.*)

obtained on a nominal beamwidth of 6 degrees over the
frequency range 40–400 kc/s.

As a final remark on the subject of non-linear systems, we
can observe that, in addition to the transmitting applications
discussed above, there are also possibilities in receiving applications. These are in the nature of highly-directive receivers
using a local high-intensity "pump" wave in the same way as
used in parametric amplifiers in electronic and radio systems.
It is not thought that these applications will prove as important

as those concerned with transmission and so they will not be discussed any further here; but already experiments have confirmed that power gain may be obtained in a non-linear (or "parametric") acoustic receiver.

4 Digital sonar systems

The sonar systems which we have discussed so far all depend for the processing of the received signals on the conventional type of electronic circuitry. In a subject as rapidly developing as electronics it is perhaps misleading to talk about the "conventional", but by this we mean amplifiers, frequency changers, filters, etc. Such electronic circuits are often called "analogue" circuits because they are definable as far as their performance is concerned by classical mathematical equations, of which they are said to be the electronic analogues. The design and construction of such circuits is reasonably well understood, and nowadays, by the use of transistors and other new components, they can be kept quite small and compact in comparison with say 20 years ago. Nevertheless, the electronic equipment for the receiver of an electronic-scanning sonar occupies several cubic feet and costs some thousands of pounds.

The rapid development of large electronic computers has, however, been the main cause of the introduction of a different type of electronic circuit system. This is known as the "digital" system. Instead of the electronic operations being definable by classical mathematical equations, in which continuous variables like x, y and z have coefficients to which particular values may be attached for a particular problem, in the digital system everything is done on a numerical basis as in everyday arithmetic, in cash registers, in desk calculators, etc. Because the most convenient type of electronic counting unit can only count in a scale of 2 (as opposed to the normal everyday scale of 10), the "binary" system of counting is used. The particular point which is important here is that all the basic electronic circuits are the same; they are simple units which go into either the position zero or the position "1" ("position" defined by electronic parameters, of course, and not by mechanical position) according to the numbers fed in.

Now these simple basic units are normally based on transistors, resistors and sometimes capacitors. All these can be

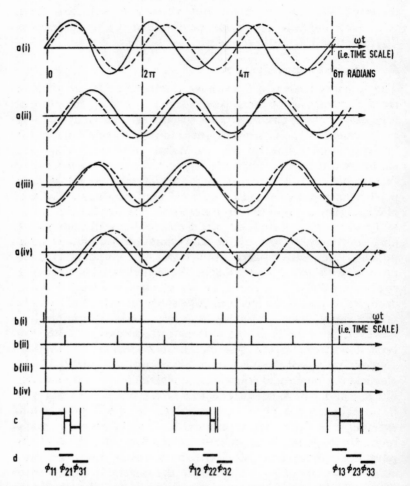

Fig. 56.—Demonstration of the principles of digital sonar. (a) Signal waveforms on four adjacent transducer sections. Dashed lines show the pure signal, full lines show the signal disturbed by noise. (b) pulses marking the zero-crossings of the noisy waves, (c) time measurements indicating the phase differences between the signals on adjacent sections—for the noisy waves, (d) the same as (c), but for the pure signals.

readily incorporated in miniature and microminiature circuit units, and vast arrays of binary circuit units can be packed by these modern techniques into volumes, not of cubic feet, but of cubic centimetres. With the development of these techniques into mass production the cost is bound to fall very low too. It therefore appeared to us at Birmingham that we should investigate the possibility of applying digital techniques to the more sophisticated sonar systems with a view to reducing their size and cost and making them more attractive to civilian users such as the fishing industry. Dr. Donald Nairn began this work early in 1962.

It quickly became apparent that merely to try to do with digital circuits what had already been done with analogue circuits was useless; this led only to much more complicated and bulky equipment because the systems had been conceived in terms of analogue processes, and for the operations involved, analogue circuits were far more suitable. It became clear that a new approach to the problem of an electronic-scanning sonar was needed—one specifically conceived in terms of digital operations. After some exploration of possibilities, Dr. Nairn developed the scheme now to be described.

The basic principle is really to do away throughout most of the system with all amplitude information and to rely entirely on the phase relationship of signals. We have all got so used to thinking in terms of amplitudes that it appears at first that we must lose a lot by dispensing with amplitude information. But work done some years ago on the "period-meter", which is a display rather like the A-scan but displaying the intervals between successive zero-crossings of the wave instead of the amplitudes of its successive cycles, showed that the phase information is not only correlated with the amplitude information (i.e. one adds little to the other, or both give practically the same information regarding the signal), but is very nearly as good information. So we start off on the new system with the expectation that little will be lost by using phase instead of amplitude.

Fig. 56 will help to show how the system is conceived to work. Naturally the electronic realization of this is another matter, but it is no more difficult than the analogue circuitry previously used. It we take a sectionalized transducer as in

Fig. 34, then, when the wave comes from a direction other than normal to the array, the signal received on successive sections is shifted in phase relative to its neighbour because of the extra travel $d \sin \theta$. This is shown for four adjacent sections at (a) in Fig. 56, where the dashed sinusoids represent the signals received when there is no noise present to disturb them. As drawn, $d \sin \theta$ is made equal to $\pi/10$ radians. In practice, however, the signals will be disturbed by noise, and the resultant waveforms may typically be as shown by the full lines. Since the noise will be usually different on the different sections, we have shown the disturbances as randomly related.

Following the transducer these waveforms are amplified (one unavoidable concession to analogue circuitry!) and then chopped so that only a very tiny fraction at the base of each half-cycle remains. This residual wave is an almost completely rectangular wave, and the only information left in it is the times at which the wave changes polarity. If this change of polarity is caused to generate a very short sharp pulse each time, we obtain waveforms as shown for the four transducer sections at (b) in the figure. Here the short pulses mark accurately the times of zero-crossing. The pulses shown in the figure are those derived from the noisy input waves.

By means of counting circuits driven by a fast "clock-pulse" generator, the time intervals between corresponding pulses on channels (i) and (ii), between (ii) and (iii), between (iii) and (iv), etc. can be measured and recorded on the digital counting circuits. These times, or "counts" are as shown at (c). For the signal without noise they are as shown at (d), where all the times are equal. This operation is conveniently done every second or third half-cycle to allow time for the circuits to operate and avoid confusion. On the first count, let the times or counts (which indeed actually represent the phase differences between the input waves) be ϕ_{11}, ϕ_{21}, ϕ_{31} as shown. On the second count, the final subscript is changed to 2, so that we have ϕ_{12}, ϕ_{22}, ϕ_{32}, etc.; and so on.

Now it is clear that if we find that all the ϕ are equal on the first count, we may safely assume there is a strong signal coming in. If this condition is repeated at the subsequent few counts, we become quite certain. If, on the other hand, we find that all the ϕ are different on the first count, and appear to be random, then we suspect that there is no signal, and only noise is being received. If this condition is found also at the following few counts, we become reasonably certain that there is no signal being received. In between these two extremes lie the more usual cases where a wanted signal is disturbed by noise. On the first count it will not be possible to decide with any certainty whether there is a signal or not, but if several subsequent counts all give a strong suggestion of signal, then we become more certain that a signal is present. After sufficient counts (if the signal pulse is long enough) we can make a reasonable decision.

The process can be expressed in terms of symbols thus. On the first count let the average value of ϕ_{11}, ϕ_{21}, ... $\phi_{n-1.1}$ (where n is the number of sections in the transducer) be $\bar{\phi}$. The difference between $\bar{\phi}$ and each ϕ is then taken, and the average difference found thus:—

$$A = \frac{1}{n-1} \sum_{r=1}^{n-1} \left| \bar{\phi} - \phi_{r,1} \right|$$

where the vertical lines are the "modulus" sign, which means we ignore the fact that some differences are positive and some negative. If a pure signal is being received, $A = 0$. The larger A, the less likely is there to be a signal. So we set a threshold and if A falls below this we retain the measurement; otherwise we assume there is probably no signal and we reject the measurement, starting again at the next count. If we retain the measurement, we still make the next count and obtain a value of A for this, then again for the 3rd, 4th and subsequent counts up to the expected maximum for the pulse duration used. There are a number of ways in which we can then examine the information, but they all amount to determining whether the sum of all the A values is small enough to confirm that a signal is present and whether the values are consistent enough.

Now all the arithmetic, measurement, and determination of whether the thresholds are satisfied is done by the digital circuitry quite automatically once it has been set up suitably; it is indeed a small, special-purpose "on-line", digital computer. If the various criteria are satisfied, so that the system "decides" that a signal is present, then the direction from which it has arrived is readily determined from the average value $\bar{\phi}$, and a bright mark is put on the B-scan display at the correct bearing. The range is, of course, determined in the usual way by the time elapsed since transmission. So we have a sector-scan display just like the earlier systems except that all targets displayed have the same brightness, much of the random background has been removed, and the operator is required to exercise much less judgement since most of the decisions have already been made by the equipment.

There is no need to have a normal display at all; since all the information exists in numerical form in the equipment, it can be printed out if desired—or this may be done in addition.

At the time of writing, no trials of an operational system have yet been made; but an experimental set has been built and demonstrated in the laboratory. In these demonstrations a synthetic target echo and noise background are used, and the effect of different threshold settings and of different signal-to-noise ratios can be shown. Some typical results are shown in Fig. 57 (page 108). It can be seen that when the threshold of A is set rather high, then many noise peaks are accepted as signal, and on a single pulse transmission it would not be possible to determine which marks on the display were true targets and which were just noise. But if the display is observed over several pulses, then the noise peaks do not recur in the same positions, but the signal marks do very nearly; the signal marks vary in position from pulse to pulse only in so far as the superimposed noise causes an error in the measurement of the average phase, $\bar{\phi}$, each time. Thus the steady recurrence of the signal in more-or-less the same position each time makes it more readily distinguishable from noise even when the threshold is set high. But when the threshold is set low, then few noise peaks are recorded at all, and if the signal marks the display it is more readily distinguished; but sometimes even the signal fails to pass the threshold due to the effect of the superimposed noise. So we have to make a compromise between "false alarms" and "missed targets", rather more consciously than in an ordinary sonar.

Some preliminary experiments with the laboratory equipment at a reservoir, using real targets in the water, have given very promising results in that large diffuse targets such as the banks of the reservoir, ridges on the bottom, etc., have shown up clearly. It was initially feared that the principle of the digital sonar would be unsuitable for the proper detection and recognition of any but small targets occurring with rather large angular separations when at the same range. It is, of course, essential to carry out full operational trials before the digital sonar can be properly assessed, and such trials are being planned at the time of writing; but the prospects seem good.

Further Reading for Chapter 3

Section 1

Other kinds of sonar system

1   R. W. G. Haslett: "A digital sonar system", *Proc. Symposium on Signal Processing in Radar and Sonar, Inst. Electronic and Radio Engrs.*, 1964, Paper No. 27B.

2   R. Bowers: "A high-power, low-frequency sonar for sub-bottom profiling", *J. Brit. Inst. Radio Engrs.*, **25**, 1963, p. 457.

3   C. N. Smyth: "The ultrasound camera—recent considerations", *Ultrasonics*, **4**, 1966, p. 15.

4   R. W. G. Haslett: "An ultrasonic to electronic image converter tube for operation at 1.20 Mc/s", *J. Inst. Electronic and Radio Engrs.*, **31**, 1966, p. 161.

5   T. Tarnoczy: "Sound focussing lenses and waveguides", *Ultrasonics*, **3**, 1965, p. 115.

6   R. W. G. Haslett, G. Pearce, A. Welsh and K. Hussey: "The underwater acoustic camera", *Acustica*, **17**, 1966, p. 187.

7   L. Kay: "A comparison between pulse and frequency-modulation echo-ranging systems", *J. Brit. Inst. Radio Engrs.*, **19**, 1959, p. 105.

8   L. Kay: "An experimental comparison between a pulse and a frequency-modulation echo-ranging system", *J. Brit. Inst. Radio Engrs.*, **20**, 1960, p. 785.

9   B. S. McCartney: "Low frequency sound sources: statement of problem and some possible solutions", *Proc. Conf. on Electronic Engrg. in Oceanography, Inst. Electronic and Radio Engrs.*, Sept. 1966, paper No. 21.

10 B. R. Slattery: "Use of Mills cross receiving arrays in radar systems", *Proc. Inst. Electrical Engrs.*, **113**, 1966, p. 1712. (N.B. Although this paper describes a two-axis scanning radar system, the principle is directly applicable to sonar.)

Section 2.1

Fish target strength

11   D. H. Cushing, F. R. Harden Jones, R. B. Mitson, G. H. Ellis
     and G. Pearce: "Measurements of the target strength of fish",
     J. Brit. Inst. Radio Engrs., **25**, 1963, p. 299.
12   R. W. G. Haslett: "Determination of acoustic backscattering
     patterns and cross-sections of fish", *Brit. J. Applied Physics*,
     13, 1962, p. 349.
13   R. W. G. Haslett: "Physics applied to echo-sounding for fish",
     Ultrasonics, **2**, 1964, p. 11.
14   B. S. McCartney, A. R. Stubbs and M. J. Tucker: "Low-
     frequency target strengths of pilchard shoals and the hypothe-
     sis of swimbladder resonance", *Nature*, **207**, 1965, p. 39.
15   R. W. G. Haslett: "Acoustic backscattering of fish at three
     frequencies and their representation on a universal graph",
     Brit. J. Applied Phys., **16**, 1965, p. 1143.

Section 2.2

Wideband receiving transducer

16   D. G. Tucker: "Arrays with constant beam-width over a wide
     frequency-range", *Nature*, **180**, 1957, p. 496.
17   J. C. Morris and E. Hands: "Constant-beamwidth arrays for
     wide frequency bands", *Acustica*, **11**, 1961, p. 341.
18   J. C. Morris: "Broad-band constant beam-width transducers".
     J. Sound and Vibration, **1**, 1964, p. 28.

Section 3

Non-linearity in underwater acoustics

19   P. J. Westervelt: "Scattering of sound by sound", *J. Acoustical
     Soc. America*, **29**, 1957, p. 199.
20   P. J. Westervelt: "A parametric end-fire array", *J. Acoustical
     Soc. America*, **32**, 1960, p. 934
21   P. J. Westervelt: "Parametric acoustic array", *J. Acoustical
     Soc. America*, **35**, 1963, p. 535.
22   J. L. S. Bellin and R. T. Beyer: "Experimental investigation
     of an end-fire array", *J. Acoustical Soc. America*, **34**, 1962,
     p. 1051.
23   D. G. Tucker: "The exploitation of non-linearity in underwater
     acoustics", *J. Sound and Vibration*, **2**, 1965, p. 429.
24   H. O. Berktay: "Possible exploitation of non-linear acoustics
     in underwater transmitting applications", *J. Sound and
     Vibration*, **2**, 1965, p. 435.

25 H. O. Berktay: "Parametric amplification by the use of acoustic non-linearities and some possible applications", *J. Sound and Vibration,* **2,** 1965, p. 462.

Section 4

Digital sonar

26 D. Nairn: "Theoretical possibilities of a digital sonar system", *Proc. Symposium on Signal Processing, Inst. Electronic and Radio Engrs.*, July 1964, Paper No. 20.

INDEX